Everything is possible.

Kateryna Armenta

KATERYNA ARMENTA

I KNOW WHAT YOU NEED TO SUCCEED

HOW TO HARNESS THE 4 SEASONS OF SUCCESS TO UPGRADE YOUR CAREER AND YOUR LIFE

I Know What You Need To Succeed: How To Harness The 4 Seasons Of Success To Upgrade Your Career And Your Life

Copyright © 2022 by Kateryna Elena Armenta

Print ISBN: 978-1-66784-486-2
eBook ISBN: 978-1-667844-87-9

This book is dedicated to:

My mom, Elena.

This book means so much to me because it means so much to you too. I am who I am because of all the love and hard work you invested in me. Everything you instilled in me will be alive and passed to your grandchildren and future generations. Nothing is wasted. Love you deeply.

TABLE OF CONTENTS

INTRODUCTION

There are probably three reasons you picked up this book. First, you want to read an interesting life story. Second, you finally decided to change your career to something different. Or maybe you just like to read, and this book somehow ended up in your hands.

Congratulations, I got you covered.

I didn't even dream of writing a book just a year ago. But I always believed that everyone has a story to tell. You just need to learn how to tell stories. In my first book, *I Know What You Need To Succeed,* I will tell you mine.

The book idea was born so quickly and unexpectedly. After I had my first son, I spent a lot of time reflecting and reviewing my life and purpose. And one day, a letter carrier delivered a parcel. I was surprised when I opened the box. Inside was *The 10X Rule*, but I did not order this book. Who did?

After talking to my husband, he said he ordered it for himself to read. That was an even bigger surprise to me because in six years of living together, I had never seen him reading a book. It collected dust for a few months on my bookshelf until one day I was ready for a new read, and picked up *The 10X Rule*.

The book has a fantastic exercise. It asks you to write your 10-year plan and goals as though had already achieved them. I picked up my journal and started to ask myself these questions:

What do I really want?

What will fulfill me?

What are my values?

To my own surprise, a list of 16 items appeared on the page almost without effort. And one of those items said: *I have authored a best-selling book.* Of course, my next questions were, *What should I write about, and can I even write a book?*

So there it was. The book had a name a year before I finally believed in myself enough to sit down and start writing it.

Have you ever thought that you are not good enough? That you cannot do anything else besides what you do now? That you are not capable of having a better career and better life? Have you ever asked yourself, *Who am I to do something big?*

All of us have these thoughts at some point in our life. I know I did and still do from time to time. But what else do I know? These thoughts do not determine what you are capable of. They are just thoughts.

This book will share my journey from being a waitress in a foreign country that became my home to being a property manager and beyond. It took me eight years, but because I walked this journey, now I can tell you how you can make it easier and faster with all the tips and tricks I had to learn the hard way. Need more help? I have life and career coaching programs that might be just what you need. Visit <u>www.ambitiouswe.com</u> to get started.

Each part of this book will present the struggles we all face in our lives and careers, and the lessons and solutions I learned that will inspire and help you to get there faster than you would on your own.

It doesn't matter what career you start in. What matters is where you want to be. Here I will cover the seasons we all go through in our path to self-fulfillment.

I called my seasons:

Waitress: The era of discovery when I was learning what I like and don't like, where my heart is, what my passions are, and who I want to be. And last but not least, I was searching for my ideal career, one I could enjoy and would make an income.

Receptionist: The era when I got my foot in the door and showed people that I was serious about growing big and reaching greater heights.

Manager: In this era, I honed my skills and strengths, and I explored more possibilities. I developed more character qualities, learned my value, and found new ways to grow.

Beyond: The era when I discovered there is more to life than just a career—there is a calling. And I hope each of you can find that one day.

If you are ready to change your career path for the better, let's begin this journey together.

And tell your inner voice, which says you cannot, to shut up!

PART I:

WAITRESS

Did you know that per the US Bureau of Labor Statistics[1], as of May 2020, there were almost two million people working as servers, of which 1.5 million were women? And of course, even in this profession, women make less than men doing the same job. The average age of a server is 30 years old.

If you are in your thirties, and if you have decided enough is enough, that you are ready for something more, I am glad you are holding this book. I am even more excited if you got hold of it in your twenties because now you have an advantage over most.

My story is from the perspective of an immigrant who moved to a new country. Even with a university education and real-world experience, I still had to start over from the very bottom.

So, it doesn't matter where you are at right now in your career path. This book is exactly what you need to start!

---

1   Bureau of Labor Statistics, U.S. Department of Labor, *Labor Force Statistics from the Current Population Survey*, Household Data Annual Averages, 11. Employed persons by detailed occupation, sex, race, and Hispanic or Latino ethnicity, at https://www.bls.gov/cps/cpsaat11.htm (visited *April 9, 2022*).

CHAPTER ONE:

ARRIVAL

"You cannot swim for new horizons until you have the courage to lose sight of the shore." —William Faulkner

I took this quote to heart several times in my life.

One of them was when, after traveling at age 19, getting my education in two different countries, and working on a cruise ship, I finally decided to settle in the country that I imagined would become my home since I was 16 years old. It was the country of fewer stereotypes, big dreams, and unseen possibilities.

Born in Kazakhstan and raised in Ukraine, I always knew my place was somewhere else. It was strange for my family, as none of them ever traveled outside the country except to Russia to visit my aunt and cousins. None of them understood why I had this strange belief and urge to see the world and live on a different continent.

I packed my bag and asked my mother to purchase a one-way ticket to the United States of America. When I boarded the airplane, I was excited about my new life and a bit scared. Actually, I was terrified. I remember my mother asking me, "How are you not afraid to take this big step?" My answer was: "I am scared, but all I need to do now is board that airplane and let it take me there."

When you are afraid, concentrate on the next step only. Don't think too far ahead. Your brain will find more and more reasons not to take action. But one small step could be all you need to set everything in motion.

WHEN IT RAINS, IT POURS

On my way to the United States, my flight was late, and I had to wait for six long hours to board the next available flight to Panama City Beach, Florida. I was exhausted and had to sleep on my carry-on, holding my purse.

I had arranged for someone to meet me at my destination. Unfortunately, I didn't have their phone number or any way to communicate that my flight was coming much later than expected. I knew they would not wait for me, but I hoped that they would get updates and still come to pick me up.

When I finally landed and went to claim my luggage, my eyes were desperately searching for a person holding a sign with my name. And to my disappointment and bad luck, I didn't find anyone. I sat down on the bench, hoping that someone would walk in looking for me at any moment. I watched as every passenger disappeared through the exit door. And now it was only me and no one else. The airport staff came to ask if I was okay and if I needed help. They informed me that the airport was closing because there were no more flights until the morning.

I said to myself, *Don't panic. Think! Think, Kateryna. What is next? You've got this. You were in difficult situations before. There is always an exit. There is always a solution.*

When facing an unexpected and stressful situation, slow down your thoughts, breathe in, and say to yourself: I got this. Then think of what you can do to fix it or make it better. Remember, worrying will keep your brain in a fog, and you will not be able to think clearly. What's done is done, and you can't fix the past, but you can take care of the now and the future.

So, I got my flip phone out. Yes, back then, I still had a flip phone, believe it or not. Maybe by the time you read this book, it will be back in style... like bell-bottom jeans. And I had some Ukrainian money on my phone plan, hopefully enough to cover roaming charges. I called my mom and woke her up at 5 am, asking her to reach out to the woman in Ukraine who had arranged my pickup from the airport in the US.

A few minutes later, which seemed like an eternity, my mom called me back and said that of course, the woman could not be reached so early in the morning.

I sat for a few more minutes, thinking, *Okay, what next?*

Then I collected my things and walked out, holding my courage with both hands, worrying that it would slip away.

To my LUCK (and I mean this time good luck), there was only one taxi left—like it was meant for me. As I mentioned before, the airport was completely empty. I hope you believe in God or something more significant and higher than us. I felt like someone, or something was watching over me at that precise moment.

I told the taxi driver that I didn't know where I was going. I asked him to take me to a hotel in Panama City Beach. I thought I would get to the hotel, rest for a night, and then figure out in the morning what was next. He asked me how I had found myself in this situation; I said there was someone who was supposed to meet me, but they didn't.

Now for the real miracle. The taxi driver asked me if I knew their name, and I responded with what I had. And he said:

"I know him. I will call him right now."

Would you believe that? My jaw dropped!

I watched him dialing the number and asking someone on the other end if he was supposed to pick up a girl from the airport.

The response I overheard was, "Oh, sh___, I forgot! I am coming now. Where can I meet you?"

I CAN DO BETTER THAN THAT

If you were born and raised in the United States, I don't think you will ever face anything like I am about to tell you. But this is my story, and I hope it could help another immigrant or anyone else who is planning to relocate to start from scratch.

I was brought to a one-bedroom apartment rented by an old man who slept in the living room. There was another young woman like me in the room and only two mattresses on the floor.

When you walk into accommodations like that, you really hope that you will be okay and that no one will take your passport away and make you disappear forever. At least that's what I thought, seeing all that. But my roommate came back from working at the dry cleaner's, and I asked her if there was anything suspicious going on. I was glad to hear that she had been living there for a month and still had her passport.

I was exhausted from 20 hours of travel, but I could barely sleep that night, hoarding all my important belongings under my pillow.

Morning came. I opened my eyes and checked that my passport and money were still there. My roommate was packing her things in a hurry, informing me that she was moving to a new place. It made me sad to know that I would be in that one-bedroom apartment with only the old man for company.

I cannot remember his name anymore, but I do remember that the old man in the living room ended up being a nice person. He fed me breakfast and asked me what I needed to do, go to the bank or buy some groceries? I told him I had some cash, and he suggested I didn't keep it on me but instead go open a bank account and get a debit card. That is exactly what I did.

Later that day, I called my contact who was supposed to help me get my first job. The news wasn't good. Because it was the middle of summer, all the positions he had were filled, and the only place he could offer me was that same dry cleaner's. I knew I could do so much better, but he convinced me to go and have a look. A few days later, he picked me up to show me the potential first job.

When we arrived, I was speechless. It was 98 degrees outside and probably 150 inside of a huge commercial garage with tons of equipment and sweaty workers all from different countries. I remember saying to myself, *NO WAY! I CAN DO BETTER THAN THIS.*

The next month, I tried to grasp any opportunity I could for a better job. I walked for miles to ask for work at gas stations. Every day I called the person who was supposed to help me, asking if there was anything new.

I promised myself that I would try to get something better before I gave in and took what was available. I had enough money to survive for about three months.

If you have a chance to give yourself a little time to find something better, wait and keep looking. Sometimes if you settle for a less-than-ideal situation, better opportunities will close the door, and it might take you much longer to move on.

From time to time, I would pick up a few shifts here and there just to have enough money for food and so I wouldn't spend all my savings. They were usually one-time gigs: serving at a large wedding, helping at an event to set up and clean tables, or covering a shift for a housekeeper that didn't show up that day.

That was when it hit me, covering for a housekeeper. I met two women who opened my eyes to what I just told you about not settling. One was very intelligent and educated, with a doctorate degree in the arts from a Russian university. She spoke English—not perfectly, but not bad at all. She had moved to the US seven years ago, started at that job, and never left. And then there was another girl similar to her, who had been there for 10 years.

When I heard their stories, I told myself I didn't come here for a life like theirs. I came for a better life and big opportunities, and I would keep looking until I found them.

But was I any different than those women? I had to prove it to myself first.

CHAPTER SUMMARY/KEY TAKEAWAYS

The tips in this chapter can be applied to life overall and to your job search as well.

Remember:

- If you are standing at the beginning of a long journey but you are too afraid to walk, take just one small step and then another one. Do you remember that turtle who made it to the finish line faster than a rabbit? Just keep moving slowly, one step at a time.

- In a stressful situation, slow down and take a deep breath. Maybe even close your eyes for a second. Tell yourself, *What's done is done, and I can't fix the past, but I can figure out the best possible solution.* You could also ask yourself a question like, *How would the person I admire deal with this situation?*

- Keep looking for a better job or solution but set a sensible time frame and do everything in your power to get what you need.

In the next chapter, I will tell you about obstacles I faced and opportunities I found right alongside the challenges.

CHAPTER TWO:

THE CHALLENGE IS REAL

"Just because you fail once doesn't mean you'll fail at everything. Keep trying, hold on, and always trust yourself because if you don't, then who will?"—Marilyn Monroe

One month later, I still didn't have a job, and my belief was shaken. I started to give in to all those doubtful thoughts and voices:

Why are you even here?

What did you expect?

You are a failure, and you will go back home as a failure….

You know all these voices that we hear in the back of our mind, trying to convince us to run from everything that is not familiar or putting us under stress? Well known, the fight-or-flight response. It is normal, and we all experience it.

But it is better to try and know that you gave it a chance than not to try and always wonder what would have happened if you did. What decision would you regret two or even five years from now? When I ask myself this question, I usually find the answer right away.

Let's get back to the story. I was feeling lonely and hated where I was living. Even the nice old guy in the living room who helped me several times was starting to make me feel uncomfortable.

At my next gig, I met this cute redheaded Ukrainian girl who said she was renting an apartment by herself and had a room for the next two months. After that, her lease was up, and she planned to move. I saw this as an opportunity to move in with someone like me and maybe learn something that could help me in my journey.

When I moved in, I was so eager for conversation and friendship. I wore a big smile and tried to approach her for a quick chat several mornings in a row, only to discover she wasn't that friendly. Sometimes she would not even respond to a good morning or hello. But eventually we became friends despite her interesting personality.

Another month dragged by with daily calls to find connections to get a better job.

One day there was hope. The guy who forgot to meet me at the airport called me and said, "I potentially have a front desk job for you. The interview is tomorrow. I will pick you up so you can talk to the manager."

That was my chance. I had no doubt that I would get the job.

THE CHANCE

We were late for my first interview. I learned afterward that he is always late wherever he goes.

I apologized, and we had an interesting conversation about my previous experience in Poland and on cruise ships. The hotel manager was impressed, I think, and offered me a one-shift trial to see how well I would do. Everything went just fine, but at the end of the shift, she asked if I had transportation and how I was planning to make it to work each evening. I explained that I didn't have a car but would do my best and use a taxi, sometimes a local trolley, or ask that same person who brought me for an interview to give me a ride. He did it for others like me for a fee. He could take me to work and even pick me up after the shift. She agreed.

About an hour after I left my trial shift, the manager called to say she couldn't hire me because she didn't trust the timing of the person who was supposed to give me a ride.

A rock smashed my uplifted mood, and my hopes just dropped to the bottom this beautiful blue ocean off the shore of Panama City Beach. I cried and cried because it was my chance to get that better job, and now I would have to lower my standards and expectations and just accept what was available because I was at the end of my financial resources. I thought how unfair it was to judge someone by another person's habits.

If you have ever lived in Florida, you would know it is impossible to exist here with no car. It is nothing like all the other big cities I used to live in, where you can go anywhere with public transportation. But here, it was obvious I needed to start thinking about getting a car to get a job to make money to buy my first car. Did you have to read that again? I had to. How could I buy a car to get to a job when I had no money because I didn't have a job? I faced that same dilemma with work experience, but we will come back to that later.

It was September, and I had arrived in the middle of June. So, it had been almost three months of my knocking on doors and looking for a decent job for an immigrant.

My phone rang the day I was packing a suitcase and looking for a ticket to go to Philadelphia to try my luck there. It was a job offer making sandwiches in Subway. If you didn't guess right the first time, I'll give you one more chance… yes, I took the job. I had to. I was about to run out of money, and on top of that, I had to move to a different place soon because my lease was about to expire.

Every day we face choices and make decisions. Each choice you make is your responsibility alone, and once you decide, don't second guess yourself. Trust yourself and believe everything that happens, happens for a reason. There is no point wasting your time and energy looking back. But it is your decision to step into your future by doing your best at everything now.

ANYTHING YOU DO, DO IT AT YOUR BEST

I showed up to my first day of work happy and excited. Mostly I was responsible for prep, and at lunchtime, I would come to the front to help serve the customers.

Anything you do, do it as best as you can. This mantra became one of the drivers that took me from that Subway job to becoming a property manager. Don't just stay on autopilot during your shifts—be curious, find what you like about this specific job, show your interest, and ask what else you can do outside your responsibilities. Believe that people will see you, and more and more doors will open in front of you.

My manager at Subway was a lovely man a few months away from retiring. Everything was so light and easy with him, and he always smiled. I loved working with him. This is what a smile can do. What a strong power it has. You probably realized when you smile at someone, they smile back. And it doesn't stop there. You can trick your mind into having a good mood and a better day if you intentionally fake a smile. Your body will start to produce the happiness hormone, and your day will become brighter.

Back to my manager. His only downside was that he didn't really want to teach me anything. Every time I asked how to do this or that, he would say, "Don't worry. I'll take care of it."

A lot of us do that when we are ready to move on or change jobs. We stop caring about what is happening and how things should be done. We start to think, *It is not my problem anymore, I don't care, someone else will take care of it.* DON'T DO THIS.

Carry out your responsibilities to the end. Even when you put your two weeks' notice in, still do the best you can. In fact, ask people who are staying on if they will help with the transition to make it as smooth as possible. Believe me, it makes a difference.

But soon enough, I was introduced to my new manager at Subway: a Russian girl who had been living in the US for several years, spoke excellent English, and was very demanding. She didn't smile very often, but unlike my former manager, she was ready to teach me everything I asked and everything she knew. It mattered a lot to me.

I always aim do my best at any job. And Subway wasn't an exception, even if it definitely wasn't my dream job.

Of course, my four-hour shifts weren't enough to make a living, so I kept looking. The next call happened a few weeks later. There was a waitressing job at the Japanese restaurant right across the street from Subway.

I was so happy that I didn't need a car, at least here. I could just walk across the street and be at my second job. I will tell you about having multiple jobs in the following chapters and how I could handle them simultaneously.

CHAPTER SUMMARY/KEY TAKEAWAYS

The first two chapters are more about life than career, but there are a lot of lessons that will bring you good results both in your life and at work.

- Don't be afraid to try something new. It is never too late for new beginnings even if sometimes you have to start at the bottom. If it feels right, there is a reason why. Just trust yourself.

- Once you make a decision, don't second guess yourself. I will repeat it: trust yourself. There is nothing worse than looking back and thinking, *What if?* It will not get you anywhere.

- And once you put your head to it (or your hands), do the best you can. It doesn't matter what it is, even something as simple as making a sandwich.

Finally, we come to the chapter where I reveal my waitress experience. Everything I learned in that season of my life could open your eyes to something you didn't know.

CHAPTER THREE:

KEEPING EYES AND MIND OPEN

"We all have to start somewhere. No one is born an actress, speaker, or architect. Anyone we become in our lives and careers has a beginning. And sometimes, we start in places that are not related to the end results we want. But if you believe and keep looking for opportunities, you will find your way to where you want to be or even to a place that will be greater than your expectations."—Kateryna Armenta

I was looking for a quote to say something like that but couldn't find one, so I wrote my own.

And so my year of working two jobs began, mornings at Subway and evenings at the Japanese restaurant. Waiting tables in the United States will usually bring you decent money because so much depends on *you* when you work for tips.

But this restaurant was not like the others. I had to split all my tips with the cooks. Don't get me wrong—it was fair because they did a lot of work and really put on a show for the patrons. But of course, when people tip you at the end, they don't know you have to split the money later, and you get what you get.

As usual, I did my best every single day and flashed my biggest smile to each customer. Some of them asked me how I ended up here and why I came. I was glad to share my little story, and many people were impressed by how bold I was to leave my home at a young age, travel, and then just decide to move on my own to a different country across the ocean. I have never thought much of it. I just knew somehow that this was my destiny.

Sometimes we have talents that we don't know about, but if you listen to what other people say about you, you will discover that your talent is in something that you do regularly, something you don't even think about. This small talent, skill, or quality could be where your mission or purpose begins.

And here is my inner life coach speaking: I suggest you do this small exercise to help you discover your unique talent. Take a piece of paper and write down everything you think you are good at and all your skills and qualities. Be generous to yourself. Then call your friends and family, or a few people who know you well, and ask them to list everything they can think of too. Combine these lists together and circle three to five skills or qualities that stand out most often or are the ones you love to use above all. Then ask yourself what career you can do to include these qualities and make another list of professions or occupations.

When I did this exercise for the first time, my own list was about 12 items long, but my family and friends came back with 20 to 30 things that I never expected. One read: "Kateryna doesn't sugarcoat, so if you want to hear what she thinks, she'll tell you like it is." My friends found this a good quality. Another common response was if they needed advice, they would not hesitate to come to me. Even my mother said that. The exercise definitely was an eye-opener for me. So, if you have never tried this before, do it today.

LEARN EVERYTHING THERE IS TO LEARN

Within a few months after the new manager started, I learned more about the Subway job. To be exact, I learned everything there was to learn: how to open the store, bake bread, prep food, handle the register, order supplies, clear down, and close up at the end of the day. But my favorite part was serving people and asking them how their day was, what they did for a living, and how they liked it.

Many returning customers knew me by name and always offered pleasant conversation and a smile. I became curious about what those people did and what I needed to have to get jobs like theirs. We often had members of the military and some police officers, whose influence led me at one point to buy and study ASVAB books religiously, planning to try myself out and see where I would fit in the armed forces. I even visited a recruiter's office once.

When you start a new job, it takes anywhere from two weeks to a few months to learn the ropes. Once you are familiar with the basics, ask your manager what else there is to learn, what could be your next step. If you start to work for yourself, don't forget that the world doesn't stop evolving, so if you want to succeed, don't stop evolving either. Look for ways to learn and grow. One of my friends said if you stop growing and developing your business, it is on the road to die. I know—harsh, but true!

The new Subway manager loved that I could cover any shift, and soon my 20 hours a week became 40.

I would start at Subway at 6 am and work till 2:30 pm, then walk to the restaurant across the street at 3:30 and work till about 11 pm after closing up and cleaning. The next day I would do it all over again. If you calculated it, you are absolutely right: that's 16 hours of work with few breaks and about five and half hours of sleep. My days "off" would be if I only had to work one job, and if I had a day completely off, it was for doing my groceries and my laundry.

I can't say that it was out of the ordinary for me. I had had experience working that much with no days off on the cruise ships. I thought of it as just another contract to make enough money to buy my first car. That car became a separate story to tell… you know that first car that you push more than you drive? Read about it on the blog at www.ambitiouswe.com under Thinking Outside the Box.

At that time, I had already moved to a new place with a room all to myself again. Yes, it was a luxury because most likely, if you were an immigrant, you would have to live with someone else in the room to afford it. I worked two 40-hour jobs and could afford to pay $500 for my own room at least, but not for my own place. Honestly, I didn't even see why I would need my own place… I had never been at home anyway.

I soon found that the place I lived in definitely didn't work for people who only have five and a half hours to sleep. It was Laketown Wharf Resort on Thomas Drive, a popular vacation spot, especially for spring break vacationers and anyone else who was young and ready to party. I definitely fit in that category, but I could not even think of going out with that much daily work. And in fact, I got the partying out of my system earlier when I had no job and would go for free—not to drink, just to have fun and dance.

My room happened to be right next to the elevators, with my only window facing busy walkways. So, every night I heard all the parties leaving and coming back again: loud, singing, laughing, screaming… I hated them. Seriously. That is probably the only time you will hear that I hated anyone.

I was sick a lot during that time, probably for about eight months straight, like every other week. I thought it was something to do with acclimatization. Probably it had more to do with being exhausted and stressed, and trying to survive. But I still had to work, because if not me, who?

BELIEVE YOU CAN BE MORE AND YOU WILL

"You are what you believe yourself to be."—Paulo Coelho

Every day I was doing the best I could at both of my jobs, and my head would spin the same thoughts over and over again.

Why am I here? What is next? I can't believe this is my life. I know I was made to be more. I have so much more to offer to this world. I know I have a big potential. What is my purpose? Is there something else I can be good at?

The Russian manager and I became friends who could talk about our lives outside of work. I shared with her how I felt and that I knew there was something else I was brought to this world to do. I just didn't know what it was. I think she understood me well because she felt the same way for herself. She is a police officer now. I am proud of her and glad she found her purpose, but unfortunately, our relationship dissolved after we went our seprate ways from that Subway.

A year and a half had passed from the time I landed in Panama City Beach, and I was still stuck in my two jobs that weren't my dream. The only part I loved was serving people and listening to what they shared with me. (Listening actually became one of my top skills on that list that I asked you to make at the beginning of this chapter.)

Some of my coworkers' career stories were discouraging. There was the woman working at Subway for 15 years, and the waitress who had been with the Japanese restaurant for eight years. They didn't love their jobs—in fact, they weren't even happy. They showed up every day kind of mad that they had to be there.

Their situations made me itchy… for real. I thought to myself, *You got to run, go and find the way out; otherwise, you will get stuck just like them. Run, Kateryna, run!* I remembered that hotel as well, and it made me itch even more.

Here I want to clarify myself. If you are made to be the best waitress or anything else, and you love your job, and it makes you happy, then it could be your calling, and there is no need to run or look for something else.

But if you are reading my thoughts and you have the same ones, it is definitely time to move on from your situation. Do it now. Because the more comfortable you get, there are more chances your brain will find excuses

not to leave your current career or life path. We naturally turn to what we know because our brain is afraid of the unknown.

A year and a half later, I still wanted to be a receptionist. I thought, *If not then, why not now?*

CHAPTER SUMMARY/KEY TAKEAWAYS

Your first job is usually not what you want or expect it to be, but it is an opportunity to discover your talents, learn new skills, maybe even realize who you really want to be, and feel ready when it is time to move on.

- Remember, each and every one of us has talents. Sometimes our talents are not visible to us, but they are noticeable by others. Don't be afraid to ask people around you what they think you are good at.
- Never stop learning, and always look for opportunities to grow and develop.
- When you hear voices in your brain say there is more for you, be ready to move and take the first step toward a new situation. Listen to this voice but not to the one that says, "Stay here, you already know everything, it is easier."

In the next chapter, you will learn how to make the next move in your career, and stay motivated and inspired for more.

PART II:

RECEPTIONIST

As you remember from the introduction, each of us has unique names for our seasons in career and in life. Mine happen to have these names, but yours could be completely different. At this step, we have a chance to get our foot in the door and prove that we are serious about growing and advancing, most of all to ourselves, but we also prove it to others by connecting with and making an impact on the right people.

Now I will tell you how I got my foot in the door.

CHAPTER FOUR:

TAKING THE NEXT STEP

"Ask and keep on asking, and it will be given to you; seek and keep on seeking, and you will find; knock and keep on knocking, and the door will be opened to you."—Matthew 7:7

Trust me, sometimes you need to knock on the same door a few times before someone opens it.

After all that time working two jobs and finally getting the itch to make a change, I took out my resume and adjusted it to "seeking a receptionist position." I started sending out my resume to all reception jobs I thought I might qualify for.

I filled out at least five applications every day, and nothing was happening... nothing, no responses at all. Now I know what I was doing wrong, and I will share with you my mistakes and the easiest way to fix them to get much faster results than I did.

I didn't plan to give up this time, but I needed to make some changes to set my plan in motion. I saw an advertisement for a TGI Fridays hostess and called them immediately, and they scheduled my interview for the next day.

I sat for the interview, and they hired me on the spot. Well, I was already 25, and you and I both know you don't need a lot of skills to be able to do that job. If you were raised in the US, you probably hosted at TGI Fridays when you were 16. Listen, I know, and you are definitely right… soon enough, I started to feel like this was not for me, like I had much more to offer. But as an immigrant, I couldn't complain. My English improved rapidly now that I was surrounded only by English speakers. Two of my previous jobs had mainly a Russian- and Spanish-speaking crew, which didn't help me learn the language I needed to be successful in this country.

Nevertheless, I did my best day in and day out, with the same big smile on my face to every guest that walked in, and it happened again. Regular people came to know me by name and always stopped for a quick chat. Here I met different types of people, all of various professions. I was glad to hear what they did in their lives and if they liked it or not. But at the same time, I felt sorry for them. A lot of them came to the bar every day to drink. After they retired, they had lost their life's purpose, or maybe they never had it, and now when there was no work to keep them busy, alcohol did.

I was in for another surprise once I left my Japanese restaurant job for TGI Fridays: I immediately got kicked out of my apartment. You see, my landlord was the owner of the Japanese restaurant. I was very fair to them, giving them two weeks' notice, but they removed me from the schedule right away and informed me that I had to be out of the apartment by Friday. To make things worse, it was Wednesday. Yes, on Wednesday, they expected me to find a new home within two days or live on the street. I panicked and cried… for a moment, I didn't know how to fix this. Where could I go on such short notice?

Then I said to myself, *They can't do this to me.* I always paid my rent on time, and in fact, I paid till the end of the month, which was in another two weeks. So, I took my courage and walked into the restaurant to talk to the owner. I said, "You have no right to do this. Just because I am an immigrant doesn't mean I am stupid. I have my rights, and you have to respect them as

I respected you by giving you my two weeks' notice. I paid till the end of the month, and I still have two weeks on the lease. This is exactly how long I am staying before I leave."

Bold, isn't it? Well, maybe it didn't sound that great. I was scared and about to cry. But I guess I shocked them because all I heard back was, "Okay." So I slowly turned around and started walking towards the exit, smiling through tears, not really believing what happened.

By the way, I found a room soon enough and even some help to move all my things.

It felt like a small win and a new beginning.

APPLICATION MISTAKES AND BETTER SOLUTIONS

Now I was living in town across the bridge from my jobs.

I still had Subway in the morning and TGI Fridays in the evening. Everything seemed to be going well. I kept looking for a receptionist job and applying for anything I could find.

My second winter as an immigrant was coming soon, which meant fewer hours at work, less money, and more free time... yay, I guess. Well, at least I had more time to look for the job I really wanted.

In the process of looking for that job, I made more than a few mistakes that cost me time and energy. I want to give you a list of all the things I did wrong and how to do them right from the get-go.

1. Figure out what you are looking for.

Like most of us at this stage in life, we are looking for "just a job," and deep down we don't know specifically what we want. And it happens not just with a job but overall in life. We might know that we want to do better, but what is "better," exactly? We have no idea. And we just throw spaghetti at the wall, hoping that some of it will stick. That is exactly what I did for several months, and that is why no one responded. And because we make so many messy attempts, most of them are low quality. Mine weren't an exception. I filled out so many applications that I didn't take time to do them thoroughly, as though I really wanted *this* job. Believe me, it shows on the other side of that application.

First, you need to figure out what job you are looking for, maybe even what company or place you want to work in. And then take time to create the best application for that specific position. Imagine yourself already taking that job, appreciate it, and write the resume to match.

2. **Create a perfect resume for this one ideal position that you want.**

Listen to what I am about to say. You probably won't agree with me, especially if you are in the situation I was in and didn't have $200 to spend on support to get a job so you could make more money. I thought the same until it finally hit me several years later.

I wrote my own resume, and it was a disaster. That resume never would have won me the job I wanted right away. In fact, it took me six months, and the only reason I got my first reception position was because few people want a seasonal job that lasts only three months.

One of the best decisions I ever made was in paying for resume writing services. No one can write you a better resume than the person looking at that resume to hire you, right? People who do it professionally know exactly how your resume needs to look and sound to make it irresistable to your next employer.

I know it is an investment! But it is well worth it. My new and improved resume landed me a job right away, and people are still calling and writing me almost weekly to offer me a position in property management. My resume is still out there on some websites. As I said, I realized it much later in my career. But you can do it now.

I actually shared my winning property management resume on my website at www.ambitiouswe.com/resume. You are welcome to steal it.

3. Go the extra mile.

After perfecting your resume and taking time to fill out your application, go the extra mile. If there is a phone number or a company name listed, give them a call. Tell them that you just submitted your application, give them your name, and say that you would love to come for an interview. Believe me, it will make you stand out, and it will show them that you are damn serious about getting that job.

Of course, I didn't do that, because I was afraid to call someone I didn't know and say, "I want to come for an interview, please look at my application."

I realized this when I was on the other side of it and was hiring my own crew. The candidate who stood out to me most was the one who delivered his resume by hand and told me that he wanted the job and would work hard. Simple, right? But that was out of the ordinary in the age of emails and the internet. So, guess who got the job? He did. And once he was hired, he always went the extra mile. Thanks, Chuck, for teaching me that lesson. Honestly, now I can't even remember if he had a resume… I think he just showed up; we talked, and then I gave him an application. Anyway, I was impressed.

I thought at first I would give it all to you here but then decided the next chapter would be a better place for the rest of my advice. For now, I will continue with my story.

WHAT DOES IT TAKE?

There I was, applying to jobs left and right, hoping that one of my applications would hit the top of the pile. The worst is when finally someone calls back and you say, "What? Who? I don't remember. I filled out hundreds of those." I am glad I didn't do that! I said, "Yes, yes, I hoped you would call me." So this time, we scheduled the interview for the same day. Once I hung up the phone, I googled "H&R Block."

The tax preparation office wanted me for their front desk job. It was my chance to prove to myself and others that I could do this.

The interview went well, and I was promised 40 hours a week starting in January. I couldn't add another 40-hour job to two others I already had. I decided leaving TGI Fridays would be wise so I could take this opportunity and add H&R Block to my American resume. Why did I write "American resume"? I had experience working in different fields, including in a hotel reception in Poland, before moving here. I even had two degrees, one in Finance and one in Quality Management, that somehow didn't count for much in this country when I first arrived. I had to prove it all again.

I called TGI Fridays and told them when my last day would be. It was all good. The manager was even happy for me.

What happened then was more heartbreaking news. When I showed up for my first day at my new job and checked my schedule, I only found 12 to 15 hours a week. *WHAT? This is not what I was promised.* I went to the manager, and she said it was all she could offer me now. Maybe later I could get more hours. I was distraught and went home crying again.

What do I do now? This will not be enough money to survive. I didn't know what else to do besides call back TGI Fridays, explain what happened, and ask them to give me a few shifts for a week. He did; I was so grateful and could not believe that all it took was asking. I still wanted and needed the experience of the front desk, but I also needed enough money to pay my bills and buy food.

It was my first winter in Florida when I combined three jobs. When everyone around me was broke and barely getting 30 hours a week, I again had anywhere from 60 to 80 hours a week with a half day off. I had always loved planners, but I literally could not function without one this time. Otherwise, I just could not remember where I had to be and when, and what I was supposed to wear—all my jobs had different dress codes.

I heard people complain that there were no jobs, that they didn't have money, that they were broke… and somehow it was always someone else's fault. I could not understand how it was possible to think that way. They had so many advantages over me; the biggest one was that most of them were from here and spoke great English… unlike me. At that time in my life, I learned a great lesson.

It is significant, at least for me. I figured out where the problems are for most of those people.

- People hate to take responsibility. It is always easier to blame someone else and complain. But you are the driver of your life. You are the one who is holding the steering wheel. And it is up to you where your life is going.

- They probably hadn't hit rock bottom yet; they were in a tough spot, but not tough enough to start doing something differently.

- They don't know what they want out of life, so they are not determined to get it.

I know I was determined enough to work three jobs for the better future that I came across an ocean for.

CHAPTER SUMMARY/KEY TAKEAWAYS

Ask yourself the question: *Why do I need it?* Your reason must be big enough.

Make it now or never. Do or die.

Do you know why married men are more successful and make more money than unmarried ones? Because they take responsibility not just for themselves but for their family too. They are determined to provide for them. I saw it work on my husband, especially after we had a child… he almost doubled his income in one year!

The solution to all my application mistakes is a universal formula. It can work on anything, not just on your career.

CG + RA + AE + PT= DR
Clear Goal plus Right Actions plus Additional Effort and Positive Thoughts will give you Desired Results.

CHAPTER FIVE:

SOMETIMES YOU JUST NEED A CHANCE

"Any time we step out boldly to make changes, we take a chance that we might fail. But the only way to get better is to try."—Joyce Meyer

I loved my new role at the front desk of H&R Block. I was good at greeting people, smiling, and working with a phone and a computer. Today I am still good at those things thanks to my experience there.

My resume was adjusted to show that I now worked as a receptionist. And as before, I learned everything I could about the position, and if I had some free time, I read more ASVAB books and learned new words from ASVAB flash cards.

I would ask people who worked with me what this or that word meant, only to find that not even people who studied here knew them. It made me feel better than when I started and had to look up every word in the dictionary.

"Surmount" means to overcome, by the way.

Do you remember I said I would not give up this time? Knowing that the job at H&R Block was only for three months, I kept looking for a full-time receptionist position.

Even if you are just passing through at your job, make sure you still give it your best effort. You never know the impact you can make and what ripple effects can do to you right there, right now.

It was backbreaking to work so many hours only to come home and make myself sit down at the computer for another couple of hours to continue the job search and application process. But I was persistent and ready to do whatever it took.

And one day, I got an email response inviting me to attend an interview with ResortQuest By Wyndham. I was impressed just by the name. I imagined myself in their uniform, greeting people at the reception. I was ready to start that same day. I felt like there was something finally happening. Someone had looked closely at my application, and now they wanted to meet me. I was 100% sure that I would get the job and that it was made for me.

I took a half day off to drive over and meet my dream job, dressed in the best office clothes I owned.

The interview was at Tidewater Resort. I followed all the instructions on getting into the four-story parking garage and then taking a skywalk to get to the main building. Just being there made me feel like I would belong to something big. I swear it felt like a dream come true.

I let the lady at the front desk know that I had arrived, and she said to wait while she notified the manager. The waiting made me nervous. By the time they called me in, I could not string two words together. Anything I said at first certainly wasn't Grammarly-approved. The voices in the back of my mind were saying, "Oh no, you're going to mess it up, this one opportunity you finally got, you're about to lose."

I closed my eyes for a second and breathed in, and when I opened them, I was ready to talk. I found the words to say why they needed me at Tidewater. We had an enjoyable conversation, and the hiring manager sympathized with me because he had worked with people from Ukraine before and only had good feedback about them.

Leaving the interview, I was sure I had gotten the job. The hiring manager gave me his business card and said not to hesitate if I had any questions. Later, I learned that almost all managers do that (I did it too), and it does not mean much. Besides, you can contact them, and most will not even respond.

TO WAIT OR NOT TO WAIT

It was the middle of March, and the tax season was almost over together with my receptionist job.

Almost two weeks had passed after my interview, and still I didn't hear anything from ResortQuest. I remember like it was yesterday—I was working at Subway that morning, but all I could think of was getting that hotel position. *Should I call? What am I going to say? Would they even remember me?*

My Russian manager could see that I was upset and could not concentrate on the job. She knew what was going on and understood me completely. I asked for a break, took my phone, and walked outside holding the card given to me by the interviewer.

I dialed the number, the secretary responded, and I said, "I came for the interview a few weeks ago and would like to talk to Mr. Cox."

He came on the line, and he indeed remembered me.

"My name is Kateryna. I had an interview with you a few weeks ago. I am calling to follow up and see if you made a decision and if there is any place for me," I said.

There was a long pause during which I realized he didn't know what to say.

"Um… Kateryna, I'm sorry, I don't think I have anything for you now."

I said from the heart, "Mr. Cox, I really need this job. You will not regret hiring me. I learn fast. Please just give me a chance."

Another long pause.

"Okay, I think I can move some people around and put you in the small building for now where you can learn. I think it will be an excellent fit for you."

I could not believe it! "Really? Are you hiring me?"

"Yes, come fill out the paperwork. We are a large company, and it usually takes two to three weeks before you can start."

"Thank you, thank you so much! I appreciate it. You will like my work."

I ran back into Subway screaming and jumping. "I got the job, I got it!"

Here are the rest of the lessons that I learned through trial and error. They might be obvious to you, but they weren't to me then, and I really wish someone had told me.

1. Prepare for the interview.

Learn everything that you can find on the internet about the company you're interviewing for. Learn names and faces, and their mission and values. Make sure their values align with yours because if not, you probably will feel miserable working there.

Prepare your own list of questions and take a notepad and pen with you.

2. At the interview

Show up 15 minutes early. If you are running late, call ahead to let them know. But try to be on time always.

Before you walk in, take a few deep breaths and calm down. When walking in, smile and shake their hand (if it is okay to do so—you know with COVID, things changed a bit).

Be nice. Sell yourself high. Tell them why they need you and why you are the best option they have.

When they ask you what questions you have, pull out your own list and interview them. You can even write down their answers. Ask anything that you want to know. You can modify the following questions to suit your position:

When would my shifts be?

How many hours a week would I work?

Do you provide insurance?

What about vacation and paid time off?

What location would I work at?

Will I have training? How long would it last?

Is there an opportunity to move up?

Do you provide any classes or pay for ongoing education?

Who would I answer to?

What is the dress code?

Believe me, it is good that you ask questions. They will think you are serious and want the job. They might even be surprised by how prepared you are. You might get the job just because of that. But please make sure your questions are relevant and tactful. Don't say something like "Can I wear jeans to work?" if you see everyone else wearing suits. But a question like "Do you have casual Fridays?" probably would be just fine.

Ask them when they think they'll have a decision and when you can call them to follow up.

3. After the interview

The next day, write them an email. Thank them for taking the time to meet with you and tell them that you hope to work for a company like that and have a manager or mentor like them.

If they gave you a deadline for their decision, call them on that day or the day after. Don't be afraid to be annoying; all you are doing is showing that you care.

Remember, they are people too. They have probably been in a position like yours and will understand how it feels.

Everyone starts somewhere.

REHEARSE

I had two weeks before my start day. I gave notice to two of my jobs but decided to keep TGI Fridays in the evening for a few days a week just in case.

Did you know that athletes use visualizations to better their techniques and become faster or stronger? I know it sounds impossible. Several studies have proven that simply visualizing a physical activity will make you stronger and better at it with almost the same results as though you were actually doing it.

I know it works because when I used to be a dancer and choreographer, I would rehearse in my mind several times a day and then just go and do the dance. I even created several dances that I rehearsed in my mind only, and then I would perform all of them as though I had been practicing for days.

I still use this technique in so many ways. Do you know what is even more amazing about it?

When I found out that I was hired, I was happy but stressed. *What if I fail? What if I get completely lost?* So, I started to imagine myself working at that hotel and how I would answer emails and phone calls, how I would greet guests, and so on.

If you rehearse in your mind for what is important to you, you are getting closer to it. Then, when you face it in real life, you are not scared anymore because you have "done" it numerous times.

Did you watch *The Queen's Gambit*? This show got my attention because the girl practiced in her imagination to become the greatest chess player in the world.

I had never thought I would speak in public. The idea itself was terrifying to me, but not anymore. Before I take the mic, I will rehearse in my mind several times. It makes me confident that I can do it. It will make you confident too.

I am telling you, our mind is a powerful thing. Do you remember in the Bible when God created Man in His image? He is the Creator of all. So why can't you believe that you have the Creator in you?

Getting back to my story, the first day I walked in to my new job, I felt like I had been doing it all my life, that I belonged there… at least for a few years.

By the way, I met my now-husband on the evening of my last day at H&R Block. He walked in to do his tax return, and I said to myself that I could look into those eyes for the rest of my life. Before he left, I gave him my phone number because it was my only chance. He had to come back, but he didn't know that I would not be there anymore. Isn't it destiny? Since then, we have been together, and I hope it will always be that way.

CHAPTER SUMMARY/KEY TAKEAWAYS

After doing the same thing for a while, we start to think that we don't know if we are good for anything else, and making a change can be difficult. But I believe putting your mind to it will give you results.

Once you get an interview, prepare for it. Make your best first impression. At the interview, ask questions. It shows that you are interested in the position. After a few days, don't be afraid to follow up. This is exactly what got me the job. No one would have remembered me if I didn't call that time, and I definitely wouldn't have gotten hired.

Imagine what situations you could run in to at work and how you would react to them. Then rehearse in your mind how it would all play out. Even practicing for some bad scenarios can help you feel prepared for them, and then at the job already react like you know what is going on and how to handle it.

CHAPTER SIX:

SELF-EDUCATION IS THE KEY TO A DOOR WITH A BETTER LIFE

"Whenever you are asked if you can do a job, tell 'em, 'Certainly I can!' Then get busy and find out how to do it."—Theodore Roosevelt

The first two weeks were my training period at the front desk of Tidewater Resort, where a girl named Alicia taught me how to do a check-in and how the reservation software worked. They had one of those old programs with a black screen and white letters where you had to know some codes to get what you needed—definitely not user-friendly but still not complicated to learn, and they had some helpful guides on how to use it.

I learned that vacationers sometimes ask crazy questions I would not expect, and it would make me freeze for a second to process what was being asked.

I had a woman call the front desk to ask what to wear to go outside…
I was like, *What? How am I supposed to know what she should wear?* All I
could say was, "This is Florida, and it is hot." Later I would get more creative
in answering questions like that.

That front desk was busy, and eight hours would go by so fast. To tell
you honestly, I struggled with language. Answering the phone, sometimes
I could not understand, and even in person, when someone would talk too
fast, I had a problem too. I would ask my coworkers for help, and some of
them would get frustrated with me. But like anything, to become better, it
takes practice, and this was the perfect place to practice my language skills
and more. I was happy to find that I could learn a lot there and possibly grow
in my career within the company.

I even found a person to look up to. There was this amazingly strong
and ambitious woman named Jennifer Frost. Every time I saw her, I would
say to myself, *I want to be like her one day.*

They transferred me to a much smaller building in two weeks, where I
managed about 30 units. In the beginning, it was boring. I didn't have much
to do, even on the busy summer days.

**One of my tips is to learn everything there is to learn in your pro-
fession, and when there is no more, find how you can grow by learning
something else outside of your responsibilities.**

I realized how lucky I was to be placed in the Palazzo building. I took
my time to deliver the best service to every guest. Anyone could see that I
would go above and beyond to serve them or listen to their problem.

Where I could fix it, I would, but when they just needed someone to
listen, I did. Because sometimes, we don't need anyone to fix it—we just want
to feel heard. Watch the short video on YouTube called "It's not about the
nail" to understand what I mean.

I realized that I had all this time that other coworkers didn't. How?
We were all paid to be there and put in our hours. But when all was quiet at
the front desk, I could waste that time doing nothing or scrolling on social

media like my coworkers, or I could learn something. My choice was always to learn something.

One of the property managers had her office in the same building. April accepted me as a friend and helped me every time I had a question. Later I would come and ask if I could do something for her, and she would give me small assignments to do with her work. I learned a work order maintenance system and how to create invoices. She even let me do some unit reports in the winter. I was glad to help, and I absorbed the new knowledge like a sponge.

The schedules of my two different jobs started to overlap, and it was time for me to say thank you and goodbye to TGI Fridays. I had to make a choice.

IT WILL NOT BE WASTED

Self-education and knowledge are treasures that can't be taken away from you. You can lose everything, but what you learn is yours, and you can use it to rebuild yourself again.

To be honest, I didn't like to study until high school when I finally realized it was to my benefit, and I needed to study as though my life depended on it. It still does. Nothing that you learn will ever be wasted. You never know when you might need it. The best part is, the more we learn, the more our brain opens up to unique ways of thinking and problem-solving.

My two years with ResortQuest gave me so much more than the opportunity to prove myself as well as learn and advance in my career—they also gave me extra time for my personal development. The management didn't mind because I always had my work done first. Then I would ask if there was anything else I could help with and go the extra mile to deliver the best service to our customers. But when it was quiet, I would learn something. I started with Spanish first, as my husband is from Mexico. Before I could speak it, I already understood about 70% just from listening when he talked. As it turns out, you can learn a lot just by paying attention.

Then one day, I got a call from H&R Block asking me if I would like to study for free to work seasonally as a tax preparer. I was impressed that I could go and learn something for free to make money for myself later. There is so much free content available, especially now. You can become a specialist in almost anything you want. But guess what: it all works the same way. Any time that you invest money in your personal development, it will pay you back more than you spent.

I agreed and signed up for a three-month-long course. Every day Monday to Friday after eight hours of work, I had to study for three hours. I am so glad I did it, even if I only worked for two seasons after I passed the exam in December, because it gave me some life skills to use in the US. (I learned later that most Americans do not even know how to do their own taxes, not even the simplest of returns. I think this is something that should be taught in school.) Guess what? I became the youngest H&R Block tax preparer in all of Panama City and Panama City Beach locations. It made me proud. This is how I spent two more winters combining jobs again.

The tax season came to a close, and spring arrived. Every day coming in to work, I felt so much gratitude for ResortQuest, the people around me, the opportunities the company provided, and everything I went through to be there.

I made more friends at work. All of them were ladies with more experience than me. Of course, I would ask them how they made it to where they were in their life.

One of these ladies worked in the back office. Though I knew she was the manager of the building, when I saw some of the work she did, I could not wrap my brain around what her position really was. There is no equivalent to what she did in my country.

One day when I walked into her office to see what she was doing, we spoke a little bit, and then she said, "I think you could be a great property manager, Kateryna. You have what it takes in terms of attitude, and the rest you can learn." I went home that day thinking, *Do I really have what it takes?*

"What do I need to do?" That was my first question to her when I came to work the next day.

The beginning seemed easy enough: sign up and pay for a two-day class, then show up and figure out the next steps. That is exactly what I did. I found the closest class, which happened to be at Gulf Coast State College, and I paid the fee. Investment… cha-ching.

They held these classes only twice a year, and I was lucky enough to find out about them a few weeks before the start of the next one.

It was August. When I showed up for the first day, I found I was the youngest woman in the class. I was 26. There were a few other women in their late thirties, and the majority were older men. I felt like some people looked at me, probably thinking, *What is she doing here?* Believe it or not, six years into this business, I still find myself the youngest woman at all the related meetings, events, and educational classes. But who cares? It is never too late or too early to do what you like.

I remember those two days of class when I had absolutely no idea what they were talking about, and nothing made sense. A lot of legal stuff was involved, which I never could understand and frankly didn't want to deal with.

They went over a massive binder of topics in two days, only scratching the surface of what you should know to pass the exam and work. After these 16 hours of education, I walked out just as I had walked in, understanding completely nothing… for a second, I thought I must be stupid.

I went straight to the manager, who had gotten me into this, with my eyes bulging out of my head. "I didn't understand anything. How can I pass the exam?" I said. But she calmed me down. She told me that she didn't understand anything either when she had gone to study. In fact, she could barely stay awake because it was so boring. She was like me and didn't enjoy legal stuff either. She said that any time there is a legal issue, she just checks the laws to be sure of what to do. She said I didn't need to worry about it, just study to pass the exam, and once I started the work, I would understand.

Her support made me feel so much better. At least I wasn't the only one who came out of that class feeling like a fool. I took her advice and studied FS720 and FS718, the huge binder, and two books that I was given. I reread it all three times before I started to grasp the terms and the larger meaning, and then two more times to think about applying all the laws and rules I had just learned. I had to ask my friend numerous times if I had understood the concepts correctly.

In the meantime, my company opened a new position. Because I was already helping with some of the work, I was literally covering everything that needed to be done at that position, doing a double job. This position had been open before, but at the time I could not apply because I had been with the company for less than six months. But now it was open again, and I had been with the company for over a year, plus I was already performing most of the responsibilities.

Of course, I said I would apply. And I thought I should get the position, no problem. After all, I was already doing the job. They would want someone who already knew the job… I thought. But I was wrong. They didn't promote me. When I went back to the manager asking what I needed to improve to earn the position and what was the reason why they didn't hire me, the answer was absurd, but what happened next was even more ridiculous.

They told me the only reason they didn't hire me was that they felt like I would move on too fast, meaning I would grow out of the position while hoping to stay where I was… I could not believe it. But I could not believe it even more when the person they hired was assigned to me on the first day to teach her how to do her job that I didn't qualify for.

I told them I was sorry, but I couldn't help them train someone for a position that I wasn't qualified for. Maybe it was not right… especially with me going the extra mile all the time. It felt like I had the right to say no. What do you think?

After that, I clearly understood that I could not grow in that company as fast as I was ready to move up. I was fired up to study more and take my exam.

The next resistance I faced was when I scheduled my exam and informed my work a week in advance that I needed to take a day off for personal reasons. First, they said they would not know until later, and then a few days before I had to go, the management said they didn't have anyone to cover my shift and could not give me the day off. I felt frustrated. These types of exams usually need to be scheduled for at least a few weeks prior, and you pay $150 just to reserve your exam spot. I know it might not seem like a lot of money, but at the time, it was. I was only making $11 an hour.

Here I learned another life lesson that I keep facing over and over again, and I had before but didn't recognize it.

When you are on your path to grow personally or professionally, you will face resistance from people around you. Sometimes it could come from the most unexpected places. By making changes to yourself, you might be forcing changes on others or putting them in uncomfortable situations they didn't expect or initiate. Like it or not, you are a part of an ecosystem.

Most of the time, when you get resistance from someone, it is not even personal. Your friends, coworkers, or loved ones are not angry with you. Most likely, they are not comfortable with themselves. Because what they knew about you is changing one way or the other, they have to adapt to it too. They could be confused or frustrated not because there's anything wrong with your behavior, but because your behavior is causing a conflict in their own reality — their idea of how the world is, the way you are. Remember this next time you face some resistance, and don't give up on your dream just because it is uncomfortable for someone else. Two things could happen: they will adapt or leave your life… and that is okay too.

My response was that I was sorry, but I could not change my existing schedule, and I had informed the manager on time for it to be handled, and if the manager herself needed to cover the desk, she could. Sometimes we need to put our foot down and stand on what is important and true.

On the day of my exam, I drove two hours to Dothan, Alabama, to take it. The people who worked there were so lovely, explaining everything, and when a computer was available, they called me in. The test was 100 questions long, and I had three hours to complete it. Believe me, it was plenty of time. The questions were less about what facts I learned and more about how I would apply them in real life and real situations. More than half of the questions went something like this: here is the situation, there are four ways to handle it, which one is correct? I don't think I was ready to apply the facts yet, as I had never worked in a real situation like that before.

As I was walking out, they gave me a paper that said if I had passed or failed. When I picked up the form, it said: FAILED with 74 correct answers. I needed 75 to pass. You probably think how frustrating that was for me… but I wasn't frustrated or upset. I was proud that I had gotten 74 correct answers, and next time, I would pass for sure.

CHAPTER SUMMARY/KEY TAKEAWAYS

Self-education is one of the keys to your growth and change. To live is to be in motion, we all know that, so why at some point in our lives do we stop learning and moving our brain? Don't be afraid to try new things; instead look at those times as opportunities to grow and evolve.

- When you are at your job, don't limit yourself to only your duties and responsibilities. Once you have learned everything about your position, get good at asking questions. Ask how you can learn something from the next level in your company.

- Understand that you can meet resistance, and it is not because someone doesn't like you or your actions, but because of how it affects them and puts them out of their comfort zone.

CHAPTER SEVEN:

GET UP AND DO IT AGAIN

"I have not failed. I've just found 10,000 ways that won't work."—Thomas A. Edison

For some reason, my entire life was like that. You know some people will get it after trying once or not trying at all. When I was younger, I had a friend who would not do or even try, and still she got what she wanted. And on the other side was me, who had to do everything for 100 times before getting it on the 101st time. I seemed to see it everywhere: in my education, my career, my fitness exercises, and so on. But I would be stubborn enough to get up and try it one more time and then one more and another one until I succeeded. My mom would say that I got it from birth.

I didn't know what she meant until I was about 15. I had heard the story before, but now I was old enough to understand.

"You are a fighter, Kateryna," my mom would say. "When you were born, conditions were so poor, and it was so unsanitary that the doctors found out you had bacteria that usually live in horses. The doctors said they were sorry, and that I was young enough to have another baby. There was no medication. You needed two doses of a specific antibiotic to kill the bacteria. Your father could only find one dose. The doctors said not to have too much hope as your body would start to reject any food given to you. But you fought through, and you were sick for your entire childhood. Look at you now! You are so strong, and there is no evidence of any of that trouble," my mom would tell me.

I guess I applied my strength everywhere in my life. If I want something, I will not stop until I get it. I am only glad I had good ideas and opportunities.

My exam failure wasn't an exception. I was going back with a plan to take two days off and then study all the books and laws for the sixth time.

It was autumn, and my work slowed down dramatically, so again I had all the time I needed to study more. I decided not to wait until I read it all over again before setting a deadline for the next exam. So I scheduled it as soon as I could. That was about one month from my first try.

Having a deadline makes you work harder and take it more seriously. It's not just true for exams; it's true in anything you do, even if you set an imaginary deadline and make a plan for it. Have you heard of setting S.M.A.R.T. goals? Read why it is important to set goals and how you can benefit from setting the right ones on my blog at www.ambitiouswe.com.

I worked and studied. It was my priority to pass that exam. And then I got resistance again from my manager when I notified her of the day I had to take off. It seemed no one could cover me again. I asked myself what was more important, to grow and evolve or to stay where I was to please others? The answer was obvious to me. The manager wasn't happy, but they didn't fire me.

The second time going for my exam, I had no doubt that I had got it in the bag, that it was just a formality. It took me about an hour and a half to finish the exam, and now that I knew what to expect from the questions, my mind was ready to tackle them with no problem.

Guess what happened next? I PASSED.

How happy my mom and I were. I felt like it was the beginning of a new level in my career.

DO NOT GIVE UP

A lot of us want to believe that as soon as we finish college, or a certification or course, we will find the job we studied for. Like it would just land in our lap. But like many others, I kept hitting a wall. Before I tell you how long it took to convince someone to hire me, I want to tell you a story that I heard at least five times from other women.

I am all for education and universities and degrees, but I am not for going into debt to have access to an education. The money you expected to make right out of college to pay off your school loans might not come for another five to seven years. You might end up paying it off almost for the rest of your life. I know it sounds hard to believe, but keep on reading.

The story goes like this.

"I took out a loan so I could study for this career that will make $$$. I studied for two to five years and ended up with a loan of $$$. But I thought it was no problem because as soon as I finished school, I could find the job I studied for and pay off the loan so fast, like it didn't even happen. Two years after I finished, I still couldn't find a job because I didn't have the experience to start working. Dilemma. When I finally got hired, I found I was not making even close to what I was planning to make, and probably it will take me about five years to get to the $$$ I expected. All the while, my debt is growing."

Why do I want to tell you that? For three big reasons:

1. Money and Debt. Try to find other ways to get an education without going into debt for it. Today, there are so many options for smaller and cheaper courses, classes, and licenses. And, of course, scholarships and grants are available for colleges and universities. In my case, I had spent only about $800 to begin with, and I could make good money at an entry-level job in my field.

2. Expectations versus Reality. Of course, we all want to find a job right away, but often it takes time, anywhere from a few months to a few years. Remember, if you give up, it will never happen.

3. If you have already gone into debt for your education, don't give up now. What is the reason you wanted to go into this particular field in the first place? Work harder to get a career in the field you want and pay off your debt as soon as you can.

I am glad I didn't take out any loans. I just saved up money from several paychecks to fund my exams. And when I passed and got my license, I thought I would get the job without a problem in the next month or so.

Well… as you probably guessed, it didn't happen for me. And it took me much longer than anticipated—seven months, to be exact.

BUILDING A DETOUR

After moving to the United States, I have always been impressed by how they build roads and bridges here. It was nothing like in Ukraine where I used to live. There the situation would always look the same: people would build and repair during peak travel times, and you would be stuck in traffic for hours. When finally passing by the work area, you would see only a few people patching the road for example. Here, every time they rebuild, repair, or add something, it seems almost effortless and has no impact on the traffic. In fact, all these years of living here in Panama City Beach, they never stopped widening and improving the infrastructure.

But what important lesson did I learn from that? Every day I would see them working on the side of the road, preparing the ground, making lanes, and starting to pour the asphalt layer after layer. When the traffic would be impacted, workers will instead work at night when there are fewer or no cars on the road. You are watching all of that happening on the side, not influencing your daily travel much at all. But then one day you leave the house and when you take your usual route, suddenly you are driving on a completely new road.

What does building a road have to do with your career?

Because you can pave the way for your new life or career while still driving on the old roads temporarily to support your current lifestyle. You will probably have to work harder on the side, and you might even work at night, but it will pay off. One day you will switch to your new life or career almost effortlessly.

Now back to my story and my seven months of knocking on doors and turning over stones.

I got my license. What was next? My resume had to be completely revamped from that of a customer service professional at the front desk to one of a property manager. They are absolutely two different resumes. Just adding new education and licenses would not work. But I hope you remember we already talked about the resume part and applications in Chapter Four.

I wish I would have done then what I already recommended to you, and hired a professional resume writer. But I guess I wasn't ready to invest more money in myself. But now I know that the best investment is you, and usually you will give yourself the best return on investment.

But I still had to get help from several people to make it more professional and fit the position I was aiming for.

I went to Debbie, the woman in the back office who already held the position I wanted, and asked her to share with me the resume that she used to get hired for her job. She agreed, and I used it as a template for my new resume. All I had to do was tweak it to fit me and my experience and skills.

Do you remember the manager who would give me additional tasks when I wanted to keep learning? That was April, and she helped me out with my resume too. She had a great way with words. She could turn simple language into a pearl. She would ask me what I did for work and my best skills and write them all down in a way that would even impress me when I reread my own resume. She did the same with my characteristics and experiences that I had never thought were special.

My resume wasn't perfect, but it was much better, and it positioned me for the job I was aiming for.

I started my application process armed with my new resume and the knowledge I learned from my first job search. I took my time on each application. I received several calls for an interview. But the majority of hiring managers screened applicants with the same question: "Do you have any experience?" I would answer them that I didn't, but I could learn so fast that they would not regret hiring me.

I went for several interviews and usually heard the same responses. "We are looking for someone with experience of at least one to three years, but we will let you know if we happen to have an entry-level position like assistant property manager."

I started to get frustrated. I didn't want an assistant position; I wanted a manager position. I got my license. An assistant didn't need a license to work.

You can't discourage me. You can't distract me. I will keep on looking, and I will find the person who will believe in me enough to hire me for the manager position, I would say to myself.

The following day, I would get up and do it all over again—apply, call, and move mountains to find that one person who would give me a chance.

Another interview was scheduled. A company in Destin needed a Community Association Manager for a high-rise in Panama City Beach.

I was so glad that, even after looking at my resume and knowing that I didn't have experience, they still decided to schedule my interview.

I met the president and CEO of Southern Association Management on a Monday morning. You know the kind of person he is when you first look at him; you understand immediately that he has a big heart. This is how I felt about Jeff Cresse.

We had a great conversation. He told me that he could not offer me the position they had because, like everywhere else, they needed someone with experience. But he told me to call him back in a couple of weeks to see if he had any other open positions for me. He gave me his card, and I don't know if he really expected me to call him back. But to me, he seemed like a person who gave others a shot. I think I reminded him of his daughter because she was in her twenties, just like I was then.

I didn't stop looking for more opportunities, but I held on to that card and counted the days until I could call him back. Two weeks later, I picked up the phone. I didn't know if he would remember me, but I introduced myself and said, "You told me to call in a couple of weeks to see if you had anything available. So here I am."

There were a few seconds of silence… and then, "I have a clerk position. Would you like to start there? As soon as I have something else available, I promise to give you a chance. But the job is in Destin. I don't know if you would want to commute that far every day. So, what do you say?"

He was right about the distance. It was a long two-hour commute to Destin, and in summer it could take up to four hours in the evening. But I had to get my foot in the door of Community Management, and it looked like a good opportunity to me.

I explained to my now-husband that I would be working and commuting long hours, but it was my chance to change my career and one day become a Community Association Manager. He understood and said that I needed to do what was right for me.

I accepted the job at $14 an hour and gave ResortQuest my two weeks' notice. They were sorry to see me go, but they didn't give me a chance to grow when I asked.

P.S. The resume that won me my last high-paying position is available for you on my website at www.ambitiouswe.com/resume.

CHAPTER SUMMARY/KEY TAKEAWAYS

Successful people are not the ones who try once and get it the first time because they just are that good. Successful people are those who simply try, and even when they fail once, twice, or more, they still get up and do it again.

You will fail. There is no other way to learn and become better. So don't be discouraged by failure. Be happy that you learned something and can now improve and try again.

Create Deadlines.

If you are studying or have a specific project you are working on, create a deadline for yourself. If you can make yourself think there is no other way around it, you will motivate yourself even more. Set up an exam date or event date, and then tell everyone about it so you feel more responsibility to deliver results, not just for yourself but for others too.

As you are reading these words, I am only halfway through writing this book. But everyone around me knows that I am working on it and that it will see the light in May. Everyone I meet will hear this from me first. It creates so much accountability with other people that I will have to deliver.

You can do the same. Don't be afraid to tell people around you what you are doing and what you are aiming for. If you don't hold yourself accountable, they will!

Don't Give Up.

At some point, you might think that you completed everything that you had to do, by finishing your education or doing the main and most critical step in your journey. But that is not the time to sit back and relax. Quite the opposite—that's the time to work a little bit harder to finally hit your goal, and sometimes you need to be creative to accomplish it.

Build A Detour.

Remember my road story. You don't have to cut everything off at once and then be more stressed out because of it. Instead, you can build your highway on the side, and when it is finished and ready, you can switch lanes overnight without feeling a single bump on the road.

In the next part, we will talk about finding your confidence, voice, and value.

PART III:

MANAGER

Two voices regularly fight in your mind. One will say you deserve more, and the other will say there is no need to do anything else because you feel okay in your old familiar position, even if it is not that good.

My voice didn't stop telling me that I was brought here for more, but what exactly "more" was, I still had to find out.

CHAPTER EIGHT:

THEY HIRED ME RIGHT AT THE DOOR

"When you come to the edge of all that you know, you must believe one of two things: There will be ground to stand. Or you will grow wings to fly."—O.R. Melling

It was another Monday of new beginnings for me. I had to get up early to make it to Destin from Panama City. The good thing was that I could spend the whole commute talking to my mother in Ukraine. It was the best time of day for both of us, with eight hours' difference.

My mom has always been my biggest supporter. She could not understand everything, but she would always say, "You are smart, Kateryna. You can figure it out, and your decision would be the best one for you."

At my new job, I had a short training and got to work as an accountant clerk. It takes at least a few weeks to get to know your new position and work environment. And I am no exception. Don't be afraid if you completely freak out at the beginning. It is normal for our brain to get into fight-or-flight mode.

When you feel like you're ready to bolt, all you need is a bit more time and someone to say, "You got this!"

I liked the job, and yet I hated it. I have always been good at numbers and math—that is the reason I studied finance at university. But I hated the routine of this kind of work, and being at the computer the entire eight hours was torture. Other clerks and office workers didn't seem to have any problem with it. But I had to come up with something else to do besides sitting at the computer.

One day, my accounting manager came to me and said, "By the way, all the paperwork that we are going through has to be appropriately filed." Then she pointed at two giant piles of paper in the corner and said, "Those too, we didn't have time in the last few months to do it." No one told me that before… and usually no one likes to do someone else's work. But I cheerfully agreed at a chance to get up from staring at the computer. And on top of that, I am a bit of an organization freak and systems lover. My manager probably thought I was strange for being so happy to see piles of work.

The next day I changed my schedule. I would spend three hours at the computer, then file for an hour, work another three hours at the computer, file for 45 minutes, and clean up 15 minutes before I left. Even if it still didn't make me love my job, it at least gave me a break.

I hoped the new manager position would open up quickly; otherwise, I would go crazy. About one month in, after I got a handle on the workload, I knew for sure it wasn't my type of job. I needed a place to learn daily, move around, and talk to people, not papers and computers.

LOOK FOR IT AND IT WILL FIND YOU

If you are seeking something and you are determined to get it, what you desire is seeking you just as much.

One morning I was at work going about my usual routine when my phone rang. I let it go to voicemail and didn't think much of it. At my next break, I walked outside to listen to the message.

The voice said, "Hello, my name is Bob, and I am with the management company from Santa Rosa Beach. April Gore gave me your phone number and said you were looking for a CAM position. We are looking for a CAM who can start as soon as possible at the building in Panama City Beach. Please call me back as soon as you can."

I was shocked! I said to myself, *No way!* I could not believe someone would call me without 100 applications and 100 knocks on their door. But they did.

Do you remember I told you to do your best at everything, and then do a little bit more? People will remember you just for that, and then you might not need a resume or cover letter because other people and connections you created will become your resume. This rule works for everything. If you own a business, practice this same discipline, and customers will flow to you without much advertising. But make sure you do it genuinely and with a smile.

So I called back immediately. "Bob, this is Kateryna returning your call."

"Kateryna, when can you come for an interview?"

"I can do only very early in the morning before work, or after work at 6 pm."

"Can you come today, after work?"

"Yes, but it will be at 6 pm."

"No problem. See you then."

I hung up, still in shock. I was going for an interview, and they seemed ready to hire me without the experience that everyone needed.

The rest of the day, it was difficult for me to work. I went over and over in my head how this interview would go and what I was going to say, and so on.

As I finished my day and got ready for a one-and-a-half-hour drive, I repeated to myself, *You got it, girl, nothing to worry about.*

Driving to my interview, the traffic was much worse than expected, and I realized I would be late—significantly late, by about 15 to 30 minutes.

I respect other people's time like I want other people to respect mine. Time is one of the most expensive things we are gifted when we come into this world, and it is our choice of how to use it.

I called them to inform them that I was running late, and we could reschedule if it was better for them. But again to my surprise, they said they would wait for my arrival. Wow, I could not believe it.

I found where to park, ran in to the building, found the elevator, and pushed floor six.

When the elevator doors opened, I almost ran in to the office.

"Hello, I am sorry for making you wait."

READY TO START?

The conversation was very short. They asked for my resume, and I handed it to this tall, nicely dressed man in his seventies, but he didn't even look at it. He asked me to tell him about my experience. I might have said one sentence or so before he looked up at me, handed me the paperwork, and said, "When can you start?"

I had to give two weeks' notice so this other company who believed in me could find someone to cover the clerk position.

I was still in shock and could not believe what had happened.

Right then and there, I filled out the paperwork, and they set my start date for exactly fourteen days later. I was going home to tell my future husband the big news, and that same evening I sent an email to my current company thanking them for the opportunity and informing them about the change.

Later, after I started to work for Bob, I asked him why they hired me on the spot. He told me that when he needed a manager for this building, he thought of his good friend April Gore. He called her to offer her the position.

And here my payoff came. She told him that she wasn't interested, but she knew someone who would be a perfect fit for him and the position. She told him how great this woman would be because… well, I don't know what she told him. But that someone, the great fit, was ME! Isn't it amazing?

The following day, I planned to speak to my boss in Destin. As soon as I arrived, Jeff came over and said, "I would like to talk to you." He looked kind of mad. When I walked into his office, the first thing he did was give me a big generous hug. It almost felt like a father's hug. Then he said, "I am so glad for you, and I wish you all the best, but you didn't even give me a chance." I thanked him for the opportunity, and he told me to let him know if I wanted to come back and work for him.

Did you see that? Whenever you leave a job, remember to do these three things:

- Treat them like you want to be treated. Give them your two weeks' notice. If they cut you off earlier, oh well. But at least you did your part.
- Do your job well till the last day and ask your management or your company how you may help with the transition.
- Don't burn bridges! Be nice and thank them for the experience.

I finished my clerk job in Destin, and in two weeks, I found myself standing in front of a high-rise, slowly realizing what I had signed up for.

CHAPTER SUMMARY/KEY TAKEAWAYS

I already mentioned it before, but I want to bring my formula here one more time because this chapter proved that it does work.

CG + RA + AE + PT= DR
Clear Goal plus Right Actions plus Additional Effort and Positive Thoughts will give you Desired Results.

When you understand your dreams and goals, you will find what actions need to be taken. Then add an extra mile of effort plus positive thoughts and a belief that you will find yourself where you want to be, or even in a better place.

In my case, when I decided to be a property manager, my formula looked like this:

CG: Become a Property Manager.

RA: 1. Take a class, study, and pass the test. 2. Apply and interview.

AE: 1. Do my best at my current job and go the extra mile in everything I do. 2. Call people and ask for the position.

PT: I can do this! Anything is possible! Nothing can stop me!

DR: I got hired with no interview and no resume. I had a resume, but they didn't even look at it.

CHAPTER NINE:

THE YOUNGEST FEMALE PROPERTY MANAGER IN THE AREA

"Don't limit yourself. Many people limit themselves to what they think they can do. You can go as far as your mind lets you. What you believe, remember, you can achieve."—Mary Kay Ash

We often think to ourselves, *I am too old* **or** *I am too young* **for this or that.** Good thing I didn't, because I didn't know the average age of people in this profession.

My first day at work started funny enough. When I arrived at the address, they told me to park in a space assigned to a manager. When I finally found it, someone was already parked there. But the tag had a phone number, so I called and said I was the new manager, and they were parked in my space. The lady was very friendly and said she would come immediately to move her car so I could park. When she came, she introduced herself as one of the owners in the building that I would start to manage.

I came up from the underground level to the street level of the parking garage and met another CAM who was supposed to oversee my work and train me. He was in his seventies but looked much younger and fit.

He introduced himself and asked me if I had an idea of what this work was about. I explained what I had seen at the other building and that I would be responsible for the building maintenance and working with owners and vendors. He said, "Okay, good, at least you understand." Then I turned to look at the building and could not believe what I had just signed up for.

The building was in poor condition, with crumbling stucco and peeling paint in several places. Walking farther, I saw more and more things that were just not being maintained. Pipes were rusted, gates were dirty, and wooden chairs fell apart at the front. The building was only 10 years old. How could this happen?

We kept on walking, and he explained to me more and introduced me to one of the maintenance crew. He was the only one on the shift and could not manage everything that needed to be done. Then on the way to the office on the eighth floor, he said, "But you don't need to worry. I will be here to help you for the first two weeks."

We made it to the office. He showed me my workspace, then another older man walked in. He wore a T-shirt and shorts, and sounded mean and not very friendly. He said, "Let's go sit in the meeting room, and I will tell you about what is going on here." In the space of 10 minutes, he dumped a load of information on me and then said, "I got to go now. Give me your phone number so I can call you when I need you."

Right behind him, Robert, the man who was supposed to train me for two weeks, left too, saying, "I will come by soon. Let me know if you need anything." The next time I saw him was a week later for about five minutes, and that was all my training. Oh well, it wasn't the first time for me and probably not the last. For some reason, I was just "lucky" this way. Some people say the best way to learn to swim is to be thrown in the water unexpectedly. Now I had to figure everything out on my own and learn how to deal with it.

My deep swim started here at this 23-story building.

ORGANIZE TO UNDERSTAND

It took me at least six months to adapt and understand what I was supposed to be doing. The first few weeks, with my brain already overwhelmed, at least 200 people came to introduce themselves because I was a new CAM. I met owners, vendors that we worked with, and vendors who wanted to work with us. Names, names, and more names. And I could remember none of them.

I started to learn about my building, all the procedures, and what maintenance had to be done. At that time, I had three people on the maintenance crew who were hired before me. And I wasn't satisfied with most of their work.

I probably could write an entire book just about how to get started in high-rise management.

There was so much that I had to reinvent and learn, from organizing all the files and paperwork in the office to showing the maintenance crew how I wanted them to do their job.

The organizing part was really important. You cannot do your job well until you know where to find everything you need (or might someday need). About a few weeks in, I was looking for some files, so I asked the board president to show me where all the files were kept, and I was taken to the storage room. When the door opened, I was shocked by what I saw. Boxes everywhere, not even stacked but just thrown on top of each other, some falling apart, and everything that once was inside now was on the floor. No years, no names, nothing written on anthing. A complete mess.

I looked at it and thought, *Okay, I need to start somewhere, and I might not know much, but I can organize this mess.* That one storage room took me two weeks to wrestle into a system. Actually, I moved everything into a much smaller storage room because once I put in filing cabinets and new boxes, dated everything, and put it all nicely together, it didn't take up much space at all.

My mission at that job was straightforward: the building needed a housewife to organize everything, just like at your house, but here I had 23 floors and a small team that I had to give orders to so I could get that building how I wanted it.

The job was definitely very new to me, and from time to time, I would call my mom to say, "Mom, I have no idea what I am doing. I just do what I think is right." Sometimes I felt like I wasn't going to make it. And she would always respond to me with something like, "I know how smart and strong you are, Kateryna, and you have already done so much that I know I couldn't have done. This is nothing compared to what you can do. I know you will be able to figure it out."

And that is exactly what I did. I figured that job out step by step. On the plus side, I really loved it. It was never *ever* boring. Every day I spent on the job, I learned something new.

When I had finally gotten the building under control, my management didn't worry much about what I was doing as long as no one complained. The board of directors seemed to like my ideas too and let me do what I felt was right.

Robert, the manager who was overseeing my work, would say to me, "You don't need to reinvent the wheel." But I disagreed with him. I hated this method of putting a Band-Aid over an issue. I wanted to prevent the issue and avoid it completely.

One of the main things, of course, is you need to have a team that understands you and your standards. To tell you honestly, I went through at least 20 maintenance people until I found the ones that understood me. They weren't perfect, but they complemented each other: what one couldn't do, the other could. Before I left, I had formed an ideal team there for two years.

I was different than the other CAMs. I was always on my feet, and I walked the building two to four times a day in the first year. Most CAMs stay in the office and don't think it is their job to do rounds. Nothing could hide from me, whether it was something that needed to be fixed or altered, or someone from maintenance who tried to take a nap in the closet.

I could go on and on about what I did there and how. If you ever decide to go into community association management and need my help, let me know.

In my time working there, I learned the basics of plumbing, electrical, cable, and fire systems; roof types, paint types, generators, machinery equipment, and much more. I got to know each and every service provider in our town: plumber, electrician, and so on.

I would continually work on improving the systems and operations of the building. One of my contributions was in putting a small TV in the elevator area that would show the main rules and regulations in a playful manner. That cut questions from guests by probably 70%, and as a bonus, they could never claim they didn't know the rules.

As a CAM, I had to get my continuing education every two years. On top of that, I as usually wanted to be the best at what I did, I decided to study even harder to get a few more certifications and designations. This was when I discovered that apparently, I was too young for this job. I am glad I only realized it after I started. In all my classes, I was the youngest woman in the room. I sometimes noticed when I walked in that people would look at me with the same question in their eyes, like, *What is this girl doing here?*

But who cared? At least I didn't. The reason I moved to the United States was because of fewer stereotypes, and if there were still some that needed to be broken, I was ready to do that. Like this one with the age thing.

I love that we are breaking more and more stereotypes, but at the same time, I still see so many people, especially women, believe lies like I am not smart enough, not tall, not young, not old, not pretty, not skinny, not experienced enough, and so on, or the opposite, I am too old, too young, too tall, too much, too skinny, too ugly, and so on, or one more, I am not like others. So what? You don't need to be molded the right way to do what you meant to do or what you dreamed about. You don't have to be like others who are doing it. There is no specific rule, and even if there is, why not be the first one to break it and be different?

What you are so afraid to do could be the purpose you were brought into the world to fulfill. And all you need is to believe in yourself enough and not care about others' opinions.

That is what I did. I thought, *Well, I could be the first Community Manager who is young and beautiful, and one of the best with more certificates and designations than anyone else.* At least in my company…

WHO SAID WOMEN SHOULD MAKE LESS?

When I started this position, of course, with no experience, they gave me the smallest salary possible. But before I even started to work, I informed them that in three months I would like a review of my salary and then again every year. They agreed.

One more lesson: Tell your employer up front about your expectations, and when the time comes, don't expect someone to remember that they had to pay you more. Go and ask for it again. Don't forget to provide them with proof of why they have to pay you more money.

Do you believe that everything happens for a reason? So, I don't know how and I don't know when I signed up for emails from a guy by the name of Josh Doody. Apparently, he is a salary negotiation coach. *Interesting, are there people like that too?* Honestly, I didn't even know. I just found his emails very informative because he tells you exactly what you need to do to negotiate a higher salary. He doesn't even know that he helped a Ukrainian girl make more money. Thanks, Josh.

Three months passed by, and I was absolutely sure that I was doing well and should be paid more for it. I reached out to my bosses with a nice email and explained to them in detail why they should give me a raise. I had met all their expectations despite no prior experience, and I was working on improving both the building and myself. It wasn't much, but they gave me an additional $2,000 a year. I said, *Okay, let me work harder and prove that I deserve to be paid even more.*

After a full year of working there, I negotiated another $2,500. When writing my next email, I told them how much I wanted and what I had accomplished in that year with a list of at least six items, including that somehow I was saving them money. Because they were so glad to have me and didn't want me to leave and go work for someone else, they matched that $2,500. I ended up with $5,000, double what I had asked for.

I kept on working, and as before, I would always go the extra mile to deliver the best service. That was one of the reasons the owners of that building really liked me. I would take my time and pay attention to small details. I always believed that small details made a difference.

In my second year, I kept doing the best I could. As you remember, I took all the additional classes and education to get some certifications at a higher level than just a CAM license. I invested in myself and increased my worth to the company so I could ask for more pay later.

And of course, after another year, I asked for a raise of $6,000 with a concrete list of all the improvements I had made during that year. I told the building president about my negotiation and, after a few weeks, I was granted another raise of $5,500.

You might ask why I was so eager for money. I knew men who were doing the same job with fewer certifications (but, yes, with more experience) and were making about $10K-$30K more than me.

At this time in the main office, where the majority of us were women, somehow a rumor started going around about my new salary. And at first, almost everyone got mad at me. I didn't understand why. But apparently, I was making more than most of the women there, some of whom had more years at the company than me. I didn't mind the hate. I don't like drama, and I try to stay out of things like that. But then two girls from the office called me and asked me how I did it. My first question was, "Did you ask for a raise?" And they both said no.

So why are we as women afraid to ask to get paid more? It made me feel like a majority of us women are some kind of charity act. I know we were brought into this world to serve others, and you are right to feel fulfilled and happy at your job. But it is also right to be paid for it and to be paid what you deserve.

CHAPTER SUMMARY/KEY TAKEAWAYS

Do not limit yourself by what others think, nor by what you think. A lot of stereotypes are engraved in our minds, and it is our responsibility to break them.

Here is a funny story I like to tell to illustrate what I mean by outdated habits.

A husband is watching his wife boiling sausage in a pot. Before putting it in the pot, she cuts off both ends of the sausage. He asks her, "Why did you do that?"

She says, "I don't know. My mom always did it."

He suggests calling her mom to ask why she does it. They call and ask, and her mom says, "Well, I don't know, your grandma always did it."

Her husband suggests calling her as well to ask the same question.

So they do.

The husband picks up the phone and asks, "Do you know why your granddaughter cuts the ends off the sausage when she puts it to boil?"

Grandma: "Do you still have my small old pot?"

Hahaha, did you get it?

Well, the reason I tell you that is because the way your parents did something might have no use for you now. So, forget about the "too old, too young, too skinny or too tall" and do what you always wanted to do—and don't forget to ask for good compensation. Because you deserve it.

But don't get me wrong… if you just started, you need time to build up to it.

CHAPTER TEN:

UNEXPECTED PAYOFF

Jesus said, "Ask, and you will receive, and your joy will be complete" in John
16:24. Similar statements are found in Matthew 7:7; 21:22; Mark 11:24; Luke
11:9; and John 15:7.

I do truly believe that there is a higher power watching over us. When
we are in need of something, it will be given to us one way or another. But I
never thought that what I am about to tell you would happen to me.

A lot of things happened to us in the three and a half years I worked
at my first CAM position.

Living in Florida, you always need to be prepared that your city could
be in the path of the next hurricane. That is what happened on October 10th
2018. Our town and many others were hit by Hurricane Michael. Several
towns were devastated, and I am glad we evacuated at the last moment. When
we came back, the apartment we rented had water inside, and the door was
blown out. But looking at other houses with no roof or entirely broken by
trees and other apartments with no ceiling, I thought we were lucky.

But you know, in Florida, when it is hot, and there is no power and no
air conditioning, everything starts to get covered in mold. So while everyone
was just realizing what had happened to them, I told my husband that we

needed to look for a new apartment as soon as possible. The only area that was less impacted was Panama City Beach. We were living in Panama City because of the cheaper housing rates. Moving to Panama City Beach meant the housing prices would double for us. But there was not much choice, and we were lucky enough to grab what was available before it was all gone, because for anything that was left over, the prices skyrocketed.

So in all that chaos, my husband and I tried to figure out where and how we would live. The building I worked for that didn't have any damages put together a GoFundMe for all the employees, including me. On top of that, a few owners decided to open their condominiums to maintenance workers whose apartments were destroyed entirely. We stayed in another condo for a week before finding where to move.

Within a few weeks, the building collected about $20K to split between four people affected by the hurricane's devastating power. They decided to split it according to each of our needs. It worked out that they wanted to pay for five months of my rent. I could not believe it.

I ended up accepting three months of rent to get us back on our feet. I donated the rest of the money to another maintenance worker who happened to injure his back and who was not able to work for a month. I felt like he needed it much more than me.

Another godsend: three families volunteered to help us move from our previous apartment to a new one that we rented. And with their help, we were able to move everything in one day. You might think we could have just used a moving company, but none was available in the chaos left by the hurricane.

That was the first time those 165 families treated me like I was family. I was amazed. Nothing like that had ever happened to me before.

But it wasn't the last time either.

THERE IS SOMEONE WHO IS WATCHING OVER YOU

During my work for that building, about two years in, we had great news. I kept it a secret for about four months… my husband and I were expecting a baby.

Everything seemed to be going so well. We were buying a house to move into before the baby came. My husband was promoted to an account manager in the landscaping company he worked for, and we had all our health insurance through his company.

Vladimir was due on January 25th 2020. On January 10th we found out that my husband's company had filed for bankruptcy and was going out of business. A few days later, we started receiving all the medical bills that had been rejected over the last three months—all my visits, tests, and ultrasounds. So I was about to have a baby and had no insurance to cover the birth. Why was this happening now? I thought we were doing the right thing and being careful as we were supposed to.

I always knew that the Universe or God, or whatever you want to call it, works in mysterious ways, and when you are in need of something, it will be provided to you. But some of us are ashamed to accept divine help because we don't want to ask for anything, or we feel that we, for some reason, don't deserve it.

My mom always taught me the same way, not to ask anyone anything, that it is somehow shameful. Maybe it wasn't her intention. But for whatever reason, that was what I had in my mind.

I learned that it is okay to accept help, especially if a person comes to you with an open heart and open hands and wants to give it to you. It could be God or the Universe sending you help, and He or It knows that you need it and you will put it to good use, or it just needs to be in your hands. Remember, that higher power sees a much bigger picture.

So that is what happened to me again. I shared my fears with one person, Chris Canoles, the president of the condominium I worked for. The next thing I knew, he had opened a GoFundMe campaign to cover my birth expenses. I didn't expect anything from him; I had simply told my story.

Vladimir decided to come on January 20th 2020. We were at the hospital at 5 am and were expecting my child any moment when I received the first transfer to my bank account. More than 60 owners participated, and a total of $13K was collected in just seven days.

I was always willing to help, but after that, I find myself more and more often opening my hands to the needs of others in the hope that I can make a difference in their lives like they did in mine.

At the time of this writing, a lot has happened, but I see The Higher Power does its magic again in times of sorrow. I will tell you about it in my bonus chapter.

WHERE BEYOND BEGAN

In March of 2020, we all knew that COVID would change the entire world. I know it changed mine too, but honestly, I found so much peace with it.

So I returned to work two weeks after I had my child. For six weeks, I was able to work from home most of the time. I had to go in to the office only once a week. Then COVID happened, and suddenly the majority of us either didn't work for an entire month or more, or worked from home. So now I could spend more time with my newborn son.

Then Florida decided that we were different and opened the state for vacationers, and of course, we got back to work. At that time, I negotiated my schedule and came back for three days in the office and two from home, while my mother-in-law helped me out and babysat Vladimir on days I had to work in the office.

It slowly dawned on me that I couldn't really work full-time in the office as I did before because now I had something much more important to do.

They did put up with me for a long time and waited for the day when I could come back full-time. But in October of 2020, they decided that they needed a full-time person in the office. They asked me to come back, but I realized it was not an option for me anymore. So the company I worked for came up with a plan B.

This was when I finally realized my value and that it should not be determined by what men think you should be and do.

Plan B was to move me to a different building. Of course, that would be okay. What wasn't okay with me was that they wanted to return me to my starting salary. They had an excellent explanation for it. They said, "Don't worry, you will only be working 20 hours a week," which made me think *Okay, I guess it is not that bad.* I will not be on call 24/7 anymore and will have more time with my family.

I had planned a vacation in December of that year, and I was supposed to switch to the new building after my return.

A few things I heard before I left made me rethink the idea that a woman is expected to make less after she has kids, or work less, or not work at all. Okay, acceptable for WHO? And why should that be acceptable? Don't we need *more* money, not less, to support another human being? I think it's acceptable if it is the woman's decision, but not someone else's.

During my vacation, I had more and more doubts about why a mother should make less money than a woman without children. Why not more? And why can't I work less and still make more? With all these questions coming to my mind, I had to make a few calls to my boss and clarify things for myself.

And in our conversation, I heard what I needed to hear. I was told that I still had to be there daily for four hours; with the commute, it didn't make sense already, but then he continued, I would still be on a salary, so I would still have to be on call 24/7 and probably would have to stay late every day. It sounded to me like I still had to do the same 40-plus hours a week but for $15K less. It felt a lot like discrimination.

I thought for one more day and gave my notice.

The lesson was learned! Don't let anyone define your value and tell you how much you should be making and why.

At that point I thought, with all my qualifications and knowledge, I was cheaping out on myself. But to move forward, I had to leave that company. It had given me my first manager position, but I had outgrown it, and it was time to move on.

It is okay to close one door so another door can be opened in front of you.

CHAPTER SUMMARY/KEY TAKEAWAYS

I want you to remember two lessons here:

1. There is no shame in asking for something or in receiving something. In fact, if someone offers you a gift or money from the heart, you have an obligation to take it. You will not take something away from that person, but quite the opposite. You will open a stream of energy that will start the flow or continue it between you. If you decline, you might be telling the Universe or God that you don't need anything or that you don't deserve it, and the energy flow will be interrupted. There is no shortage of anything in our world, but it does have to move and flow to stay alive. So why not become one of those receivers and vessels of energy?

2. Don't let anyone tell you how much money you should be making. I will repeat: There is no shortage of anything, including money. So only you can decide how much you should be earning, and don't cheap out on yourself.

I will come back to some of these ideas in the next part and explore them more fully. Are you ready to get to the most exciting part of the book?

The last two years of my life were magical. They opened my mind, and I started to see the world differently.

P.S. Writing this, I realized that the number 2 shows up more than 100 times. It makes me think that it has to mean something. I hope it is not that this book will be sold twice, but hopefully 2 million times. Thinking positive.

PART IV:

BEYOND

When it comes to careers, there are three types of people.

The first type is people who change careers every three to five years. These people are fast-moving, and once they feel there is nothing else for them in their career, they are ready for change.

The next one is people who change careers every 10 to15 years. They will stick to their career for longer, and usually not until their late thirties or early forties will they feel the need to try something new. Their previous job doesn't make them happy anymore, and they are on the lookout for a different experience.

And one more type, people who will hold to one career or one place of work for their entire life. They stay in the same company from the day they start working to the day they retire. You probably will see fewer and fewer people like this, especially in the younger generations.

I am sorry—I forgot about one more type: people who can't hold down a job for more than a few months. But this type is due to different phenomena, and these people need to start with some deep work on themselves.

I am not 100% sure yet, but it does seem like I belong to the first type.

When I left my CAM career, first I needed to pause, take care of myself, and spend time with my child. I felt like I had worked more than I needed to for the first year of his life. Additionally, my mental health needed a significant slowdown, review, and reflection to understand what I wanted to do next.

Sometimes, we need to stop and take time off when our situation doesn't feel quite right. We need to regroup our desires and actions to be ready to fight for our happiness and ideal lifestyle. Just make sure to give yourself a time frame for it, and don't get stuck in inaction or fall into depression. The line is sometimes very thin.

In stillness and peace, my reawakening began.

CHAPTER ELEVEN:

INVEST IN YOURSELF

"There is no more profitable investment than investing in yourself. It is the best investment you can make; you can never go wrong with it. It is the true way to improve yourself to be the best version of you and lets you be able to best serve those around you."—Roy T. Bennett.

Unfortunately, as women and especially mothers, when we are busy filling everyone's proverbial cups, we forget our own. I am sure you have seen women who let get lost in motherhood after having children, not realizing that by having their cup empty of happiness and positivity, they can't fill anyone's cup with the same. What actually starts to happen is we let ourselves down, stop taking care of ourselves, and don't feel happy and fulfilled anymore. Then on top of all that, we feel guilty because we are "supposed" to be happy to have brought a child into this world, and we "should" want to take care of him or her.

My story was similar during the first year of my child's life. I tried to be the best mother and the best wife and the best housekeeper, absolutely forgetting to be the best Kateryna first. And it is no secret that going about life this way will burn you out sooner or later. It took me one full year to break myself into pieces inside. The worst thing was that my husband didn't see it and didn't understand it. But don't expect men to comprehend what you are going through. Men are wired differently. You need to communicate your feelings, your inner struggles and sorrows, but don't expect him to understand you completely. In the same way, not everything a man goes through can be understood by a woman.

What is next? How did I break through the hole I had dug for myself? My transformation started by asking myself the right questions.

What do I need to change to feel energized, happy, and myself again?

What do I need to do differently to be able to get my life back?

Why is it important to me and others?

My answers were simple enough.

1. I needed to return to the gym, not just to exercise, but to spend time with myself and others. It would motivate me to lose extra weight that was definitely making me uncomfortable and self-conscious.

2. I was hungry for self-development and internal growth. I decided to satisfy those desires with books, so my answer was simply to read.

3. I needed a community of likeminded people who wanted to grow together and support each other.

4. I felt like I had something to share with the world. But I wasn't sure what exactly it was or how to start, or where. I needed to get know myself again and rediscover what I was passionate about.

That last one was difficult to know how to fulfill. It was around the time I picked up that book, *The 10X Rule*. I finished it in only five days. It felt like my mind cracked opened a door just to peek at what was going on outside. But I needed more encouragement to come out.

Reading that first book made me feel like I was on to something... I kept on going. I was so eager to find the answer I had been looking for. And after years of searching, for some reason, I felt I was now so close. In fact, the answer had been inside me all along. But now was the time to find it and bring it to the surface.

In the next two weeks, I swallowed a dozen books. Crazy, isn't it?

I say "swallowed" because this is exactly how it felt. My brain was hungry and looking for much-needed food. And all those books came to me like a sweet fruit of knowledge I needed to nourish my mind. And when I consumed it, my eyes opened wide.

Now, it was no surprise to me why Eve wanted that fruit of good and evil. She knew that breaking the rules opens up new possibilities and widens our perspectives. After all, God created her curious and wanting to know more. And Adam had nothing else left but to blame Eve.

I see it this way: even Woman was created from Adam's rib. In the beginning, she was a leader. But because she was, God said to her that from now on, she would be in control of her husband, who would rule over her.

At that time, I asked myself probably 100 questions, and any answer that would come into my mind, I would write in my notepad. In two months, my entire notepad was filled with things I didn't know about myself before and tons of ideas for the future—and not just the ideas themselves, but plans to make them happen.

What I didn't know was that I already had what I was looking for, and it was within me and in front of me. I coached myself to find all of that in my mind. And I tell you this: it felt so good.

MASTERMIND GROUP

There is a saying, alternately attributed to the Buddha and the Theosophists, that goes, "When the student is ready, the teacher will appear."

By some kind of magic, a friend called me and said I would be a great fit for this mastermind community of young Kazakh women. Even though I wasn't Kazakh, they wanted me to join.

So I did. I liked the idea a lot because for me, one of the missing pieces in my life was a sense of belonging. I saw the potential of group support. That move made me think about how I could use the idea to make it bigger and more interesting.

Now a part of the mastermind group, I was forming my thoughts on how this kind of support should work and how I could help women better implement something similar.

You probably heard another saying, "Two minds are better than one." What is even better than two? Five or six people who want to grow together, who have different skill sets and viewpoints, and who are ready to push each other further in their development.

I stuck with this fantastic group for almost a year. It is no secret that they helped me tremendously. We instantly became fierce friends, and we still are. But at one point, I realized it was time to move on. The rule in the group was that we didn't get upset when someone left; we knew it could be for reasons of growth or that the person was not ready to put the work in. Either way, it was always for the best.

While I was still a part of the mastermind group who helped keep me on track and move faster toward my goals, I created a community to empower women to feel confident, find meaning and purpose, not underestimate themselves, and know their own value. I knew what I wanted to create, but I didn't know who I was in relation to this community and what my role should be.

I would post ideas, speeches, and articles to my new group. A few of my friends commented that they were so proud to see me grow from a waitress to a life coach.

Life coach? Am I a life coach? I didn't know anything about what life coaching was.

Funny thing though… I google everything, but the idea to google "What is a life coach?" didn't visit me for at least four months. I am glad because I might have quit before I started, now that I know how many life coaches are out there.

I think there was a great reason for that. I had four months to cook my idea independently with the help of several books on coaching. One of them was *Make Money as a Life Coach* by Sally Miller and Melissa Ricker. It was very straightforward, showing me step-by-step how to start a life-coaching business.

I won't say I'm perfect, but I always do my best at everything. Honestly, I don't even know what "perfect" is. Is there a guideline or a specific recipe for anything you do the first time? When is it ever going to be "perfect"? I think "good" is a sign that you are on the right path.

I knew I had to get certified as a Life Coach. This was my next investment in myself. I loved it: new people, new community, and I saw how different professions use life coaching in so many ways.

Of course, I didn't stop there. I take interesting classes or attend an event at least once a year to develop my skills. Neuro-linguistic programming (NLP) training is coming along too. But my responsibility now is to grow and learn more so I can help my clients in the best possible way.

I ended up hiring my own life and business coach. I know it sounds funny, a life coach for a life coach. But when you believe in what you do, you will seek the same services for yourself, like my photographer friend who would hire a photographer anytime she went on a trip to someplace new.

Did you read any of Jen Sincero's books? Two things she repeats, again and again, are: LOVE YOURSELF and HIRE A LIFE COACH.

And she is 100% right.

BEST WAYS TO INVEST

Throughout my entire life, the most expensive item I have ever owned is me.

I say this not because human life is the highest value, but because literally, the most money I invested was in myself. And it pays off every single time, one way or the other. I want to share with you all the ways you can invest in yourself and how it pays off.

One more thing before I start. What I learned and saw, especially from the time I started this book, is that you might own a lot of things, but disaster might come, and you can be left with nothing but yourself. What then will help you to build yourself up again? The answer is everything that you invested in yourself, things that don't require a bag, luggage, or car in order to take with you. The bonus chapter will explain more about what I mean.

Now, you can find numerous articles on ways to invest in yourself. But most of those articles miss a few items. My list below is the easiest to remember.

Your Body

It is difficult to feel happy, be successful, or enjoy life when your body is sick, so investing in your health should be #1 on your list.

There is no secret to it: eat whole, nutritious foods, exercise regularly, get enough sleep, and follow a daily routine.

<u>Consume less sugar. Watch your calorie intake.</u> With all the delicious drinks available to us in our modern world, a lot of times we don't think about how much sugar and calories are in just one drink. Take this example:

Smoothie King The HulkTM Strawberry: A large (40 oz) contains 1,928 calories, 64 g fat (26 g saturated fat), 250 g sugar, and 50 g protein.

I know these numbers might not mean much at first glance. But put it this way: I need about 1900 calories to maintain my current weight considering my type of work and activity level. I am 5'9" and weigh 160 lb. For 1900 calories, in one day I can eat a turkey and cheese omelet, toast with butter, pasta with chicken, beef stir fry, and peanut butter and banana on toast… or I could drink one smoothie. But we all know that would be impossible because it doesn't matter how much you eat; in four or five hours, you will be hungry again.

Another common culprit: we all love coffee, and the place to go for one is Starbucks®. But how about having an entire meal in just one drink of coffee? Something like their Salted Caramel Mocha Frappuccino with 550 calories and 90 g sugar will do.

As for exercise, it doesn't have to be anything crazy like marathons. Of course, feel free to challenge yourself. But even simple walking, yoga, dancing, gardening, swimming, or fun group classes will keep you moving, energized, and happy. Pick something that you enjoy so that you will stick with it more easily. I don't always feel like exercising, but I will get up and do it anyway so I can check off my "body investment" box for the day. If you don't know how to start by yourself, hire a trainer. You will get double the motivation when you put skin in the game to have someone screaming in your ear that you can do it just one more time.

Last, make sleep a priority in your daily routine. You know when a child doesn't have a routine, and they get cranky and whiny? Without a routine, a child feels insecure because they don't know what to expect next. Creating a routine for your child will make life so much easier for parents. My son has a simple daily routine. He does the same things at the same time every day, like clockwork. And I usually don't have any problems with him. In the evenings, I put him in bed, give him a kiss, say goodnight, and walk out. That's it, all done.

Now, believe it or not, routines continue to work for us throughout our lives. If our schedule is all over the place, we will be cranky, stressed, depressed, unhappy, and the list goes on. But having some kind of structure will reduce your stress level and keep you happier overall. You know I am all about schedules, routines, and habits because they are easy, and they work!

Your Mind

Here I can give you a long list (now you know that mindset work is kind of my thing…).

Learn constantly. I hate to see a woman or a man who cares about their body so much and looks fantastic, but when it comes to conversation, has nothing to say. They are empty…. So how come we fuel our body, but we don't fuel our brain? The average American reads or listens to one book a year. Just one. Because "we don't have time," but we do have time to pointlessly watch stupid reels or videos on Facebook, TikTok, Instagram, and whatever comes next. A 2021 statistic shows that we spend 145 minutes a day on social media on average.[2] Most people read about 40 to 50 pages an hour… so I guess you don't have time to learn and grow….

Reading a book (or listening to one) is just one way to learn. If it is not for you, and you prefer someone to teach you, take a course instead. There is a course available on literally any topic. Find one that will help you grow or learn new skills, one that will teach you something you can implement in your work to make it better, more productive, etc. Courses can even be easy and fun: try webinars, workshops, and events. Those have so much to offer. You get not only new information, but also ways to use it, and even networking that might be useful in the future.

Languages can train your mind well too. Start learning a language that you always wanted to speak or understand.

Important! Don't forget to implement what you learn. There is nothing good about *knowing it* if you don't *use it* to better your life or the lives of others. If you don't use your new knowledge, you will soon forget it.

<u>Write more.</u> Writing will give you so many benefits: stress release, creativity, and curiosity, to name a few. Try a "brain dump:" take a pen and paper and write down everything that comes to mind. Among the ideas you wrote down, you will find, of course, a lot of duds, but you might find several gems too. Don't know where to start? Get a journal with guiding questions already printed inside. A life coach could be a great resource as well, not just

---

2 Djordevic, Milos. "Global Social Media Usage Statistics: How Much Time Do People Spend on Social Media?" *Letter.ly*, 26 Apr. 2021, <u>letter.ly/how-much-time-do-people-spend-on-social-media</u>. Accessed 11 April 2022.

in writing but in speaking your thoughts and ideas out loud to someone who won't judge.

If the above is not for you, start with daily schedule writing, budgets, and anything else that may be tracked and recorded.

And yes, I say to use a pen and paper. There is much more to the mind-body connection than you think.

Create. Once a year, I would pick a project that I had never done before, something creative, and I would do it for a few months during the slow season at work, when I had more time for creativity. I have completed a lot of different, interesting projects. Most were some type of handicraft. But I never guessed that my next creative project would be book writing. So create something, anything, even if you think you have no talent for it. You might discover something you never expected from yourself. You don't know if you will be good at it until you try.

Travel. Get out and discover something new outside of your usual environment. We get our inspiration from the world around us. Seeing new places, learning about new cultures, and trying new things will widen your imagination and open new horizons.

Don't think about buying the next most expensive pair of shoes, but think instead about how to plan your next trip to places you have never seen. I can 100% confirm this one after visiting 21 countries and still trying to add a new place to my list every year. Don't limit yourself to one country. There are 194 more to see.

Find a mentor. For that matter, find several! Think about people you admire and can look up to. Meet them for a chat. Can't meet? Find other ways to learn from them.

Hire a life coach. It is no secret that most successful people have a fitness trainer and a life coach. That is why successful people keep getting even more successful—they know which tools to use. After only a few sessions, you will start looking at the world with new eyes, and some kind of awakening will begin inside you.

Make sure you don't forget about your body by doing all or some of this! Your mind is connected to your body, and you need to remember to take care of both halves.

Your Spirit

I am not sure where to start here.

Do you believe? I don't mean in God, but do you believe that there is something higher than us people and this earth? My belief could be different than that of Christians or anyone else.

I believe that there is a higher power and that it is all ONE and the same, so it doesn't matter how you call it. There is no right or wrong religion. That higher power has had different names and faces throughout human history. I believe as well that we are all connected, and we all resonate with the entire universe, not just our planet, but it goes beyond into what we cannot understand. I know that knowledge comes to some people, and they are called to share it with others.

Find your belief. Did you know that in the worst of times, when we have no control over the situation, so many of us, even those who never believed in God, start to pray? Why is that? I know I did it when my mother was getting emergency heart surgery. I prayed as hard as I could. When war started in Ukraine on February 24th 2022, up to the time I am writing these words, I prayed more than I ever did. We need someone to look out for us and to be able to hand over our pain and our worries for someone or something to handle.

Philippians 4:6-7 "Do not be anxious about anything, but in everything by prayer and supplication with thanksgiving let your requests be made known to God. And the peace of God, which surpasses all understanding, will guard your hearts and your minds in Christ Jesus."

Remember, there is someone looking out for us. I know it. I have proof.

Find how you want to call it and believe that you are not alone.

Give to others. I heard this once, and I thought how powerful it is: "When you hold onto material things so hard with your fists closed, there is nothing else that you can take, because your hands are full. But if you open your hands and share with others your blessings, your hands will be open, and you may receive more blessings." We are made to give and to care for others, and these are part of our spiritual journey too.

Keep track of your feelings and energy. Did you know that you can train yourself to have positive feelings and emotions? By doing that, your energy output to the world changes, and the world changes with you. So it is up to you to shape the kind of world we are all living in, and for that, we all need to take responsibility.

Your Relations

Why is this an investment in you? There are two reasons why.

Communication skills. By improving your communication skills, you can take the next step in your career and in your life. Remember, nothing is wasted, and the skill of communicating can take you to new heights. Everything is built on relationships, so why not strive to make yours the best? That is all I have to say for now on this one because I am myself a student and want to learn more and become better.

Networking. The right connection may change your life forever. You could be at the ground level of your journey, but the right connection may take you straight to the top floor. So go and meet people. Talk to others, listen, become interested in what they want to share with you, and remember their names. (If you know me, this sentence probably makes you laugh—I am horrible at remembering names. I have to repeat a name at least five times before I remember it. But I am trying out this new habit: when I meet someone, I will repeat their name several times in the first few minutes. I try to do it in conversation so I don't look too weird, but sometimes I still do by repeating it to myself before the person leaves my sight!)

Remember, you are the only thing that you can control in the world of chaos.

CHAPTER SUMMARY/KEY TAKEAWAYS

Don't feel bad or guilty when you invest in yourself. Everything that you put into yourself will only make you grow higher and shine brighter, and you may discover your talent, calling, or passion along the way. Investing in yourself will bring happiness and meaning into your life. Let's talk more in the next chapter about why passion is so important and how to find it.

CHAPTER TWELVE:

FIND YOUR PASSION

"Happiness is not in the mere possession of money; it lies in the joy of achievement, in the thrill of creative effort."—Franklin D. Roosevelt

There is no one on Earth who doesn't want to be happy. So if we all want the same thing, why is it still so difficult to get?

Every single human was brought to this planet with some specific mission or assignment. We are all looking for it, and we call it a career. Some people get lucky and know from a young age what they are meant to do. But for the majority of us, it takes decades, and some people end up asking themselves that question before they die without fulfilling their purpose.

Do you remember when you were asked in school, "What do you want to be when you grow up?" I know we all had an answer ready. But of course, we grow up to find ourselves facing unexpected situations and either rethinking our answer or losing it altogether. Years go by, and we get so busy with life that we forget about our purpose.

But if you recently asked yourself the same question again, **What do I want to be when I grow up?**, *not everything is lost. Your mission and your passion are still calling for you, and it is not too late to start looking for them.*

I KNOW WHAT YOU NEED TO SUCCEED   93

I asked myself this question several times in my life. As you have already read in the previous chapter, the last time was after I had my child. I had to support it with other questions to really dig deep. Surprisingly it happened when I still had a steady job that I thought I liked. But there was still something waiting for me to discover.

When I wrote and wrote in my journal and found my passion and my Why, everything changed. I finally realized what I needed to do.

I took to heart this question: if you knew you were dying, what would you want to be remembered for?

The reality is we spend about 90,000 hours of our lifespan working. We need to work because this is how we contribute to our community and the world. So now, if we spend so much time on something that we are not happy or passionate about, or even hate, does this poison our life? The answer is yes. It spreads just like a disease through your life and through your body. And then we keep on infecting the life around us.

What gets you so excited that you forget to eat? That could be your calling or your passion, or at least where you can begin looking.

Did you ever meet any artists? Looking into their eyes, you can see how passionate they are about what they do and how that brings life and energy into them and everything around them. They might not be rich with money, but they are rich with happiness.

And this phenomenon is not restricted to artists. You can meet a hairdresser, barista, or server who has that light in their eyes that will tell you in the first few seconds they love what they do and are passionate about it, and that is why they are the best. The line for their services never gets short. They get excited every time to do their job, and they will do it the best way possible.

MONEY OR PASSION

When starting our career journey, we often have to ask ourselves this question:

Money or passion?

When I was 19 years old, I loved to dance. I was so passionate about it that I became a self-taught choreographer. With that passion, I taught in three countries, and dancing became my side hustle. When I had to choose between my passion and money, of course, my parents convinced me that dancers couldn't earn enough for a living, and I went to do what I was good at but not passionate about—finance and accounting.

I am sure I'm not the only one who heard that from their parents or other family and friends. But is that even true? Why do we believe that doing something for money has to be better or different than doing something for pleasure and from the heart?

Do you remember me saying that we are all brought here with a specific mission? So now imagine that about 50% of people hate their jobs, which means they're in the wrong place and possibly taking someone else's spot, who might love to do what they are doing. Don't for a second think it is impossible. If there are undertakers, coroners, and forensic pathologists who love what they do, then there is someone to love your clerk or accounting job that you hate. Why don't you leave it for them and find a place where you feel happier and more passionate?

The good news is that the number of people who hate their jobs is decreasing. So it seems like we are finally able to break through some limiting beliefs about money and passion, and more of us are sticking with our gut on what we should do in our lives and doing it with passion.

Don't get me wrong here. It takes time for most of us to realize what we love to do and what we are talented at. That is why our life is a journey during which we can learn and discover our possibilities and potential. If you had to change your job or career in the process of discovering your true passion, that's normal. But what I ask from you is that you don't get stuck at the job or career you absolutely hate or feel is not what you were meant to do. Keep on searching.

How to start and where? Questions, questions, questions. There are tons that you can ask yourself to dig deeper. Here are just a few to start you in the right direction.

1. If money were no object, how would you fill your time?

2. What do you find fulfilling or important in life?

3. If you were the richest person on the planet, what would you be doing with your time?

I know that maybe you were tempted to answer that last question with "Nothing… I would just enjoy life and travel" or "Lie at the beach and have drinks." I understand you might want to do that if all you did last year was work hard at the job you never liked. But how long could you really lie on the beach? How long could you really do nothing? If you stay stagnant for more than a few weeks or months, you will start getting bored, your life will lose meaning once again, and you will end up back at square one. So ask yourself that question again.

PASSION IS LIQUID

We may mistakenly believe that our passion has to be in one specific type of job or career. But passion is liquid. It may transform and flow from one job to another.

I will use myself as an example to explain what I mean.

From a young age, I loved to dance (and still do, by the way). But I never was that perfect dancer with impressive splits. What I loved most about dancing was creating something in my brain and then projecting it onto others and telling them how to deliver it in an even more incredible way. Some moves that I had in my mind I could not do myself, but I could tell dancers how to make it perfect with the right feeling and emotion.

Years went by, and I was still able to do this as my hobby from time to time, even outside of the world of dance. The jobs that I liked were always about creating something and teaching others how to deliver it. I did it at the property management job too. It might look like the job of a CAM is all about laws and rules, but it takes a whole lot of creativity to figure out how to put these pieces together to make them work.

Realizing my next step in life and opening the door a bit wider to my calling is still that same pattern. I like to create, deliver, and watch people's lives change.

So what is it that you like to do? Not what you are good at but what you genuinely enjoy even though you are not perfect at it and don't know everything about it. Now in what career can you apply it the best and still be okay with everything else that comes with the job?

Talking to my photographer friend and how she came to her passion, it was interesting to hear that her passion accounts for only 10% of her entire work. The rest is what she is ready to put up with to enjoy that 10%.

Everyone has their own reason to be passionate about a certain profession. Let's take the medical profession for example. One person could be in it because he or she likes to solve problems and use critical thinking, and the other one to serve people in some meaningful way. But they are both ready to put up with the rest of this career for that one driving element they love.

Food for thought: something that you are good at but don't like doing is not your passion, but it definitely may be applied to those things that you have to deal with. And your hobby is not necessarily your passion but possibly your outlet.

CHAPTER SUMMARY/KEY TAKEAWAYS

"Build your own dreams, or someone else will hire you to build theirs."— Farrah Gray

A woman once said to me, "I wish I had met you 15 years ago because now it is too late for me to change anything." First, it is never too late, and what if this is exactly the right time? Second, 15 years ago, I hadn't walked my journey yet and didn't know everything I do now. If we keep on learning, the journey never really ends. So what if this is the beginning of yours?

Proof is everywhere that age is not a barrier. Carolyn Doelling decided to become a model after she turned 70—and became sought-after in the fashion industry. Julia Child became a household name as a celebrity chef after writing her first cookbook at age 50. Anna Moses, a housekeeper, started painting at 78 years old and went on to sell her work for $1.2 million.

Still unsure if you have time to find your passion and be successful at it?

Why don't you take the first step and see what happens? Because if you are looking for it, it is looking for you too, and all you need to do is start.

CHAPTER THIRTEEN:

WHAT DO YOU WANT?

There are some lucky people who get their way easier and faster without having to work much for it. But the most successful people are those who work for it… a lot. Of course, we usually don't see the work that was put into something day in and day out; what we see are results. Then we think, *How lucky they are. It is so easy for them; it just falls from the sky like manna.*

It is easier to assume that someone is simply luckier than you, and that you don't get anything your way despite all your hard work. You may even hope that someone will come and sympathize with you over that. Let's admit it: the majority of us are lazy, and we only do something if we really need it or if our life depends on it. That is why men are at their best when they are trying to get that perfect woman they saw somewhere; they will do whatever it takes to get her—100 calls, 100 flowers, carrying her backpack, and so on.

But when it comes to daily life, we are plodding along, hoping to catch a current that will carry us somewhere without effort on our part. When it does, though, we are surprised to find ourselves nowhere near where we wanted to end up.

After starting my life coaching business, which is a journey of consistency and commitment, I found out that so many of us have no idea what we want in our lives. You can't arrive somewhere when you don't have a destination. You may have great experience but still end up completely lost. How often do you board a plane, train, or even a car without knowing its destination? I don't think it happens that often. You might try it once in your life, but most of us want to know where we are going so we can prepare.

Nevertheless, we do it all the time in life. We board a train and just hope it will bring us to the beach or the mountains or somewhere else nice and that we would have everything we need there. Doing so, we too often end up on the North Pole or somewhere on the side of the road without a map and a guide. Could you prepare and take the map with all the steps and checkpoints? Sure... but first, figure out where you really want to go.

I know it sounds easy enough... we usually have an answer in the first two seconds. "I want happiness, love, peace, success!" But the follow-up questions make the majority of us look like a deer in headlights. What is happiness, success, peace for you? Can you describe your day, week, month, year in that state? Usually, that's getting people to think much harder, and sometimes they will find a meaningful answer, but sometimes that seems like too much work and they give up.

So, if you want to live that happy life, you need to determine what it even means to you. Crazy enough, you might already have the majority of components to put it together, but you never realized that they were there. Those things that make you happy could be already in your possession, but without taking an inventory, you will never know whether you are halfway there or whether you still have much to attain.

Start asking yourself the right questions today! Hire a life coach to help you.

GOAL SETTING

Sometimes, it is so difficult to understand what you truly want, but it is the first step in drafting your map to success.

Most likely, it will not be a straight line from point A to point B. It might look more like a labyrinth, treasure map, or even tree roots that will have some different outcomes but still take you to that desired level.

Why get clarity on what you truly want? I have a few reasons that will give you immediate benefits.

1. Your anxiety levels will drop, and your uncertainty will go away. The unknown keeps us awake at night. But when we know what is there for us tomorrow and 10 years from now, we always sleep better.

2. You will instantly start to feel happier. Wow… I know that is how I felt every time I had a specific goal to work toward. Goal setting might help with finding your bigger purpose. It is all connected.

3. You will feel more confident in making decisions because you know where you are going. No more floating through life on autopilot.

4. You will value your time and others'. It will dawn on you how little time you have and how much you have still to do. Your time will become an expensive thing, a luxury, and you will think much more wisely about using it.

5. You will treat drama and distractions just like background noise, and they will not affect you anymore.

What do you want in your life? What should you do today to make it the best day possible? Where should you be a year from now? How can you be better on yourself tomorrow, and how can you be better for others?

And remember to start your questions with what, where, and how to allow your brain to seek an answer. Then listen, and write it down. You will start to know and understand yourself better, and you might just find what you are looking for.

WHY DO YOU WANT IT?

My Why was so clear to me from the beginning when I decided to open my own Life Coaching practice.

I want women to know they have a choice in their lives. My purpose comes from seeing my mother, my sister, and other women around the world who so often think the opposite, that they are obligated to serve someone else's decisions. And so often, women trap themselves in living for the desires of those closest to them, like parents, friends, or husbands. They are tied down by thinking they have no choice.

My mother recently shared her experience living with my father. She said:

"He tried to bend me and fold me into this extreme, uncomfortable way of living. And every time I thought it was my fault, that I needed to be a better wife, a better mother, and just be what he wanted me to be. So, he would bend me once, and it hurt, it was uncomfortable, it itched, but you go on like that, and you adapt to this shape. But then the next time comes when he thought it wasn't enough, and I would be bended and folded again. And it is horrible, painful, and uncomfortable, but you think you have no choice, and you get used to this shape once more. But when all your bones are broken, and you are not you anymore, there is nothing left to break and bend, and you get discarded. And you are left to realize that you are a broken, uneven shape of self who doesn't know who she is. But what if I could choose me, and bloom and grow like a nourished flower?"

Now she thinks that she has been broken so many times that she is nothing but a wilted flower on the ground covered in dirt. But do you know what wilted plants are good for? To fertilize new growth, which alone could be her purpose.

I heard so many stories before that now I want women to make their own choices. Choices they want, not choices they were forced into by someone.

This is my Why! It is strong enough for me to know that I may change the life of one woman who wants to make her own choices.

I have my second Why, and it is my family and my child. I think that would be true for every mother out there.

So what is your Why that can keep you going for your goals and finding your passion and purpose?

One more note about finding your Why. Every time I talk about mine, it grabs my heart to the point of almost crying. That is how deeply I connect with it.

What grabs your heart?

CHAPTER SUMMARY/KEY TAKEAWAYS

There is no one out there who can answer these big questions for you. The only way to start drafting your map is to figure out what you want and why. And when you are ready to follow your map, do it with dignity and respect for other people's Whys. Every path and every story has its own right to exist. Don't think that yours is the only correct one. Your map might be valid for you but not for everyone else. Not many of my friends and family can understand my Why, but it does not matter. What is important is that it gets me every time I think about it, and from there, I know what I need to do.

Do you?

In the next chapter, I will talk about what got me this far. It might not look like success to you. But I know it is success to me. Because success is not comparing yourself to others, but comparing yourself to yourself—yesterday, a year ago, five years ago.

CHAPTER FOURTEEN:

IT TAKES COMMITMENT AND CONSISTENCY

"The only limit to your impact is your imagination and commitment."—
Tony Robbins

As I said before, nothing was gifted to me like manna from the sky. In fact, I was born and became a weak, sick, skinny child who would barely speak when asked a question. My mom would often ask me if I had just woken up. My voice was so quiet that she could not hear me…

At 12 years old, during summer break, I grew almost five inches. My back muscles were stretched so much that they could not hold me up straight anymore. My mom became concerned seeing me walking around like a hook. Even when she corrected me 100 times a day, it didn't last long enough. Of course, as any concerned mother would, she took me to the doctor.

The news was a bit disturbing: my right leg was an inch shorter than my left, and my back muscles weren't ready to hold me up. The doctor prescribed some vitamins, but the primary treatment was exercise; otherwise, I was looking at life with horrible posture and other health issues. I remember he looked at me and said, "Girl, it is only your choice to fix this, or not." I walked out of his office, shocked and speechless.

To give you a little bit of background: my family, like most others, worked hard to pay the bills and put food on the table. So I barely saw my parents at home; they were always working. My mom simply didn't have time for me.

So she was not going to take me to exercise three times a week. The next day in the evening, I told my mom that I heard of an aerobic class 25 minutes away from our home on foot, and I would go and see if I could join it.

I walked into the class like a lost girl, and everyone looked at me like, *Did you forget something?* It was not a friendly atmosphere. But I came back the next time and the next. I did it for four years before switching to dance—and I am still doing it. It has been 20 years now. That is what consistency and commitment look like. Commit like your life depends on it, and do it as long as it takes to succeed.

I truly realized how important that was when about five years ago, I ran into this woman I knew. I remembered her, she was a year older than me, and we used to play together when we were girls. She was beautiful then, tall with long, dark hair and lovely eyes. At about the same age as me, she had had the same issue I did. She grew way too fast, one of her legs was shorter than the other, and her muscles were weak. I don't know who missed the point in her family, but when I saw her all those years later, that poor young woman had her back so crooked and folded, and her leg was about four inches shorter than the other.

I saw what could have happened to me if I had not decided what needed to be done, to commit to it, and then to consistently do my exercises. This is how life-changing commitment and consistency could be—the compound effect at work in full force.

How often do we announce that we are going to take action, and then we do it for a few days and leave it, or simply don't do it at all?

How many times did you tell yourself that you are going to change your habits but give up after the first Monday? Because right, we all start on Monday—or next month, or next year.

But if someone told you that behind a door lies everything that you want, would you wait till Monday, next month, or next year to open it? Probably not.

You will not succeed at anything if you don't commit to follow through.

Want to lose weight? Follow a meal plan for 30 days at first, then 90 days, and then review what you are eating daily.

Want to look fit? Commit to exercising—daily, weekly, monthly, and so on.

Want to become an author? Commit to writing from the beginning of your book to the end.

Why do we fail? Because we don't commit fully. We make excuses. We think, *Yes, I am on a diet, but I am going out with a friend, so I will just eat it this one time.* Another one: *I am reading a book but didn't finish it because I got too busy.* And so on.

What if there were no other choice? What if you were to think, *If I don't do it, then there is no future for me.* Would you look at things differently?

Commit to it with your entire body, soul, mind, feelings, heart, and everything else. Because if you don't, there is no reason to believe that it will work out if you do it just once or twice. What is the point of starting if you already know you aren't committed? You are setting yourself up for failure. Because that is what you will get. There can be no change without commitment first.

What works best for me is to commit to one goal at a time. If I can make it a habit, I will feel able to commit to another goal. But if it is a goal that needs to be reached in a specific period, you will hear me say no to everything else until I have completed the goal I am currently committed to.

So what do you need to think or believe in order to commit to your goals? And what reward do you want to see at the end to make up for all your efforts?

BE CONSISTENT

"Do it again and again. Consistency makes the raindrops to create holes in the rock. Whatever is difficult can be done easily with regular attendance, attention and action."—Israelmore Ayivor

Everything I have achieved in my life is because of two things, commitment and consistency, and you will hear me saying this a lot.

When I decided to study English in order to come to the United States for the first time, I studied the language for nine hours a week every week for three years—156 weeks, or 1404 hours, to be exact. I knew what I wanted, and I decided to make it happen. I won't lie, the first year was tough. I was the worst in the class and sometimes could not understand a thing they were talking about. I know many of my peers judged me or thought I was stupid. At times I wanted to agree with them. I thought I was not capable of learning English. Then one day, it clicked in my brain. It felt like a switch was finally turned on. Some people quit along the way, and I remember only a few out of 10 people made it to the final exam. And because of my 1404 hours of consistency, I became one of the best graduates.

Once again, it proved to me that to become good at something, you need to do it long enough. You might start as the worst, it might take you longer, but you might find yourself the first—or the only one—to cross the finish line. And even making it that far would be the win that propels you to believe nothing is impossible, and if you did it once, you can do it again in any realm.

When I decided to write this book, I said I would do at least one page a day. I had to do more on some days to make it to the deadline that I set for myself. But for 40 days in a row so far, I have sat down for an hour or two to write. I may have upset some people by disappearing to chip away at this manuscript... but if you are holding a finished book in your hands, it means I kept a promise to myself, and it's all thanks to commitment.

I once heard, "You can succeed at anything if you do it long enough." If you started and don't see results yet, don't get discouraged. You have not been doing it long enough to make it a successful operation. Keep going until you get what you want.

CHAPTER SUMMARY/KEY TAKEAWAYS

If you get anything from this book, I want it to be this:

SET A CLEAR GOAL, COMMIT TO IT, AND CONSISTENTLY TAKE ACTION TOWARD IT.

Let's talk about confidence in the next chapter. What is it, and where do we get it?

CHAPTER FIFTEEN:

DEVELOPING CONFIDENCE

"I want you to know that you are good enough. That every time you give your best, it is enough. Once you stop worrying about what others think and instead focus on yourself, your life will change for the better. You deserve to be confident in who you are and not worry about what other people think."—Kateryna Armenta

Being confident does not mean you are cocky, arrogant, or conceited. Instead, confidence is the belief that you have what it takes. Confidence allows you to be vulnerable and admit your weaknesses for the sake of improvement. It also allows you to be authentic and true to who you are without worrying about what others will think.

Do you remember that scared little girl from the previous chapter who spoke too quietly because she was afraid to be heard? Yep, I'm talking about myself.

My mom says, "I can't believe how strong your voice is now and how firm your opinions are; you don't feel afraid to speak up for what is right to you."

It took a lot of practice, but every time I chose action instead of fear, my confidence grew another inch. *The Confidence Code* by Katty Kay and Claire Shipman explains that we women weren't born with confidence, unlike men. Men, not women, are wired to act. But we can grow and develop our confidence in two simple ways. First, the more you do something, the better you get, and the more confident you become. Second, every time you need to take action, stop overthinking and just do it. Make the first step, even if it is clumsy, even if others would judge. When you make that first clumsy step, be proud of yourself because it takes courage to make it. It is so much easier to sit back and judge than it is to take action.

I know my confidence is 5'9" tall, just like me, sometimes even taller. It shrinks when I encounter the unknown, and I push myself over the edge once again to grow it back.

SHOW UP RULE

This is my favorite rule that helps with both confidence and consistency.

The rule is very simple, and any time I use it, it takes my confidence further. For it to work, you need to schedule your activities to know what is happening when. Even if it is for gym classes, have a plan for what needs to be done. Then when you feel lazy and your brain tries to find 100 excuses (The weather is bad, I am tired, I can go next time), *tell yourself,* **All I need to do is show up at my best in this specific moment.**

What it does for me is it makes big things smaller… like much smaller. All I need to do is show up. The rest will happen on its own. For the gym class that you are too lazy to go to: just show up. Then you might as well work out; you're already at the gym. For the meeting that's got you scared and insecure: just show up. Then you're already there, and you have to say something and participate.

What can simply showing up do for you? First, every time you push yourself over the edge of something new or unknown, or something that you are scared of, you grow your confidence half an inch or more. I know, we don't like admitting to ourselves that we're scared; we find a reasonable excuse.

I remember my first scheduled podcast recording. I was anxious and had a mix of different feelings, good and bad. Yes, I could cancel, and that would be it. Pressure's off. But I chose to show up. In my opinion, it went great at the time. I don't know now. I might listen to it today and think it was horrible, but on the day, I showed up and did my best, and it was enough. For you too, a day will come, and your confidence will stand as tall as you or possibly even taller. All you need to do is show up.

Second, showing up will help you with consistency, and that, as we said, will give you the results you want.

Next time when your brain is looking for excuses, say to yourself, *ALL I NEED TO DO IS SHOW UP*. That is a simple task that anyone and everyone can do.

Can you do this for me? Or even better, do it for yourself. You will be glad you did.

COPING WITH CRITICISM

We all know that it is already scary enough to start something new and step over your fear.

Have you ever seen that overweight person who decides to get it under control and comes to the gym every day to walk an hour on the treadmill? I did, several in fact, and every time I thought this person had some courage to come and face the problem daily in full view of everyone else. Criticism, or simply the fear of criticism, may kill our courage at the beginning of our journey. Some people are not ready to face it and would quit after hearing one stupid opinion—an opinion, by the way, that doesn't matter.

Remember, there are two types of criticism: constructive and projected. To put it simply, there is good critiscism and bad criticism.

Constructive criticism, at one point or another in our growth, is necessary. It is good when it comes from a person who did something similar, and you definitely know that it is a reliable source. Usually, that type of criticism is easy to spot because it will sound simple, concrete, and relatable, something like: "I see how much you are working on it, but I see this one area that I think could be improved by changing this to that." Often, constructive criticism is delivered with a smile and comes out of a genuine desire to help a person grow.

Projected criticism, however, is absolutely different and should be completely ignored. It is an emotional response to something you did or said. It may be triggered unexpectedly, and it is nothing personal. Bad criticism is simply a projection of a person's psyche. It's the result of anger, insecurities, and unfulfilled desires and wishes. You can detect projected criticism in the first second or two. The person will be irritated or angry. There are those who will always have something to tell you—how to do it better or that it is just wrong altogether—but usually they never do or try for themselves. They are just always ready to give you their angry and unsatisfied opinion. Avoid people like that! I hope there is none in your circle. I know in the time of social media, it is difficult to avoid these people completely. But remember there are always about 10% of people who would offer empty criticism simply because they see you succeeding.

Here are some pointers to help you cope with negative critics if they arise on your journey.

1. Not everyone is right.

Some opinions should not matter to you at all because they are not your people to impress.

2. Setbacks are a part of every journey.

They will happen sooner or later, so just let them go! Do you remember that resistance I talked about in the earlier chapters? It is a normal part of your personal growth.

3. Know your priorities.

Putting yourself first is sometimes the best way to stay motivated and focused on what you're doing. Know your path and don't forget to refer to your map when you need to. Do you see any stops for irrelevant opinions? Then step over them and keep on going.

4. Some people won't like you no matter what.

Some people won't like what you're doing. Some people won't like the way you look. Some people just aren't that into you. You can't satisfy everyone. Remember that. That is it.

5. Learn to let go of things that don't matter.

It's a waste of time to get angry or frustrated over something that doesn't matter, and it will only slow you down. So breathe in and say something like, "I breathe in LOVE and breathe out FRUSTRATION." Thank the person for their opinion and tell them that you will do what you think is right. If you have to, cut them off or block them.

If you want to respond to projected criticism, you may need to develop a thick skin. Having a thick skin will allow you to become more resilient in the face of negative feedback so that it won't affect you as much. You'll also learn to see the bigger picture and be able to move past bad criticism much more easily.

If someone is unkind to you, it probably means they have a lot of issues and are trying to pour them onto you, so just be firm in what you're doing and remember that it is their own problem to fix. They have to work on it on their own or get help from a professional.

CHAPTER SUMMARY/KEY TAKEAWAYS

Just as making it too safe to play for our children will not teach them what they are capable of and what they should avoid, the same goes for grownups. If we play it too safe and stay in our comfort zone, we will not learn what we are capable of and what potential lies within us. Try, fail, get up, and try again until you succeed, and then do it a thousand more times to be the best you can at it.

I love my mom for that. Every time it was so difficult for her to see me standing in front of such big risks that she never would have taken herself, but she still let me go for it every time. She cried and suffered and worried and lost sleep, but she let me explore my possibilities. This is what great parenting looks like.

Explore your possibilities, show up, get outside of your comfort zone, and grow your confidence inch by inch.

In the next chapter, I will tell you why this book became so important to me and my family.

BONUS CHAPTER:

WHY THIS BOOK BECAME SO IMPORTANT

On January 31st, I was told that I needed to start this book now and have it finished within two months. I don't know, a voice in my head said my words would somehow be important to others. I work a lot, and I am a wife and a mom to a two-year-old. I never thought I could add another item to my daily list of to-dos. At first, I pushed it aside, thinking later I would have more free time to dedicate to this. But the voice did not stop—it became louder and louder. I gave in on February 12th and vowed to write a minimum of one page a day. I said I could try my best to finish it by the end of March, then try to figure out the next step to publish it. Once the decision was made, things started just magically falling into place, as though I had pulled them to me like a magnet. I found several editors, cover designers, and others who knew the ins and outs of publishing and were willing to share their expertise with me. I also got some great books in my hands that told me what I needed to know.

But there was still a gap! I didn't know why and for whom I was writing this book.

The first 10 days, I made more progress than I had expected. I was working on it with a determination that for whatever reason, this book is important. And...

Chaos, horror, and evil covered Ukraine in the night of February 24th . When I woke up in the morning, my husband told me the horrible news. I grabbed my phone to call my mother to find out if they were alive... yes, this is what war is. You don't know if you will be able to talk to your family from one minute to the next. I can't explain to you what feelings I had. My heart was squeezed, and my brain was foggy because there was nothing else I could think of. And I know I am not alone in it, and here my story is nothing in front of people who are there fighting and trying to save their lives or getting separated from their family, and there are other people who are hurting much more than I can ever imagine.

I prayed and prayed. For two weeks, I could think of nothing else, and there was not much I could do to help besides donating money, praying, and speaking my truth. But I kept writing even if I could only squeeze out one page. I felt like it was even more important now. I had to keep going. Why two weeks? As conditions on the ground worsened, my family finally decided to get all the women and children and flee to Poland. I felt some relief. They were safe. But my heart and my prayers are still with Ukraine and the people who remained as well as those who are now displaced.

The day my family crossed the border, my gap was filled. I realized who I started this book for. It was my sister who would have to start her life all over again, just like I did when I stepped on United States soil and decided to make my home here.

IF YOU DON'T BELIEVE IN GOD OR SOMETHING BIGGER, IT IS TIME

On March 6th 2022, my family finally decided to leave Ukraine and go to Poland to look for safety. They are in one of the refugee camps as I am finishing this book.

There was one day when my mother called me and said they needed $500 for all the paperwork and housing. I asked her if she needed me to send it. My mom never wanted to take anything from me, so she said they could scrape together the money and not to worry. That same day I was at work just going about my daily tasks. A lady came to pick up some documents from me and handed me an envelope. I didn't think much of it. Other people had given me cards with prayers that I appreciated a lot too. But this one was different. When I opened the envelope, I saw $500 inside with a note that said, "It is for your mom for her needs."

This was no accident. This was not luck. I didn't talk to anyone about it. It was just between me and my mom. But the Universe or God does amazing things. Keep your heart and your mind open to it, and you will start seeing the bigger picture. You will find your purpose, your Why, and the courage to fulfill your destiny.

As of March 23rd, there are more than 3.4 million refugees who left Ukraine, and they are all women and children. Maybe that is why this book had to come into the world at this specific time.

On March 24th 2022, President Biden announced the United States would welcome up to 100,000 Ukrainian refugees. Now I hope to see my family here soon and offer them some feeling of home.

CONCLUSION

As you remember at the beginning of the book, I told you we all have the same four seasons on our way to success, and they may carry different names. I called mine Waitress, Receptionist, Manager, and Beyond. We all go through these stages in our lives and in our careers, sometimes even several times. Or we get stuck at one of the levels and just walk back and forth, afraid to take the next step.

The person standing in the way of your dreams is YOU. There will be moments when you want to quit simply because you are tired, but before you accept defeat, think about your goal and why it means so much to you. Do not let what others say or do distract you from your purpose. Remind yourself of all that you have overcome and all that stands between you and success. There will be times when you get discouraged or feel as though you are not going to make it, but each time, stand in front of the mirror and give yourself a pep talk. You are not alone, and you are much stronger than they know… you just have to believe it is your time.

A life worth living is a life that is dedicated to positive change and a bright future. You've come for a reason, and you have to figure out what that reason is. The reason might make itself clear in time, but you have to be willing to go after it. If you want this future, then you need to make it happen. Start now and do something about it. Your dreams are in front of you every day, but they will never come true if you don't do what it takes to get there. If you are not willing to do what it takes to achieve your dreams, then they will find a new soul to be gifted to in order to come true through someone's else mind and hands. Time is running out, so take action and make it happen.

The moment that you decide where you are going and why it is important to you, things will start to fall into place. You are ready to move forward for a reason. Your life can become meaningful and fulfilling by making small changes in the way you think and behave every day. And it is never too late to start. It ain't over till it's over. So you can stay where you are, or you can take a chance and see where you end up.

THE CHOICE IS YOURS!

P.S. I hope you enjoyed this book, and I hope that maybe something finally clicked for you, or maybe you were reminded of what you already know, and now you are ready to act on it. I am a first-time author and would appreciate your review of this book. Thanks for taking the time to read it.

ACKNOWLEDGMENTS

I want to thank my mother above all—she is my light and my beginning.

But I have so many more people to mention here, and not just in helping me to write this book, but for being a part of my journey and teaching me those things that I needed to learn.

My best friend, Irina Lenko, always supported me and helped me brainstorm ideas. She is also the photographer for the cover art.

All the ladies from the original mastermind, go after your dreams. You can do this.

Evgeniya Stetsenko, my client, proved that I am moving in the right direction.

April Gore, Thomas Cox, Rob Berdenier, Debbie Bullock, Marina Walker, and Jeff Cresse were people who believed in me and helped me to grow in my seasons.

My husband for his patience in letting me put so much time into this work.

There are many more people who played a role in my life, whether good or bad, and because they made me who I am today, I am thankful for them.

ABOUT THE AUTHOR

Kateryna Armenta was born in Kazakhstan and grew up in Ukraine. Already at 16 years old, she fearlessly stated to everyone that she would be living in the US one day. At the time, no one among her family or friends could believe what this young lady had planned for her life.

She graduated in Ukraine with a financial degree and in Poland with a Quality Control Management degree before traveling the world, working on cruise ships. She traveled to the US for the first time when she was 19 years old and spent a summer in New Jersey working as a lifeguard. When she returned home, the sparkle in her eyes changed forever, and now nothing could stop her.

In 2013 Kateryna decided to move to the United States to settle. She found herself managing condominiums and homeowners associations. She has been a successful Community Association Manager for over four years with several certifications and designations until one day she found her true calling in helping women to discover their potential and become ambitious boss ladies who take control of their lives.

She got married to her husband, Marco, in 2017 and had her first baby boy in 2020. She continuously learns new things and loves to keep her life organized. Planning is her strength.

She wants to empower women in her community and worldwide to achieve their goals and live the life they deserve.

Now she is the founder of Ambitious WE Life and Career Coaching. You can find more information at www.ambitiouswe.com.